Effective Classroom Management

John Bryson
Series Editor: Professor Trevor Kerry

Interactive Teaching Skills

Hodder & Stoughton

A MEMBER OF THE HODDER HEADLINE GROUP

Note on Series Editor

Professor Trevor Kerry is well known for his books on the practice of teaching. He was formerly a senior LEA Adviser in charge of in-service training, and more recently has been a consultant and lecturer on aspects of education management. He holds a Visiting Fellowship in the University of East Anglia, and is Assistant Dean of the College of Teachers. He sustains his contact with the classroom by teaching on a regular basis and is an Ofsted trained inspector.

Orders: please contact Bookpoint Ltd, 39 Milton Park, Abingdon, Oxon OX14 4TD. Telephone: (44) 01235 400414, Fax: (44) 01235 400454. Lines are open from 9.00 – 6.00, Monday to Saturday, with a 24 hour message answering service. Email address: orders@bookpoint.co.uk

British Library Cataloguing in Publication Data
A catalogue record for this title is available from The British Library.

ISBN 0 340 72086 7

First published 1998
Impression number   10 9 8 7 6 5 4 3 2 1
Year   2004 2003 2002 2001 2000 1999 1998

Typeset by Transet Limited, Coventry, England.
Printed in Great Britain for Hodder & Stoughton Educational, a division of Hodder Headline Plc, 338 Euston Road, London NW1 3BH by Cox & Wyman, Reading, Berkshire

Contents

Statement of principles

The books in this series are based on a particular philosophy of teaching, which was largely developed (but not fossilised) in the 1980s as a result of the Teacher Education Project in the Universities of Nottingham, Leicester and Exeter – of which the series editor was Co-ordinator. This philosophy has stood the test of time and, it is argued, better meets the needs of teachers as professionals than some more recent developments, such as some competence models, which tend to trivialise the art and science of teaching. The principles of this philosophy are as stated:

Practical teaching consists of skills

- Skills can be isolated and identified
- Skills can be broken down into component parts
- Skills can be studied and taught
- Skills can be learned
- Skills can be reflected upon and refined
- Skills can be evaluated and assessed.

Each book takes a particular teaching skill and uses the latest research and practice to illuminate it in ways of immediate interest to all teachers.

Editorial: Skills for the future

The pace of change in society is constantly accelerating. This change is reflected in the world of education. Indeed, Drucker sums it up like this:

> *Every few hundred years in Western history there occurs a sharp transformation ... Within a few short decades, society re-arranges itself – its worldview; its basic values; its social and political structures; its arts, its key institutions. Fifty years later, there is a new world ... We are currently living through such a transformation.*
>
> **(Drucker, P (1993) Post-Capitalist Society. New York: Harper Business, p1)**

> *What will be taught and learned; how it will be taught and learned; who will make use of schooling; and the position of the school in society – all of this will change greatly during ensuing decades. Indeed, no other institution faces changes as radical as those that will transform the school.*
>
> **(Drucker, op. cit. p209)**

Yet it could be argued that even these changes have been modest in scope and pace compared with the changes that are likely to occur in the early years of the twenty-first century. Already the portents are visible of events which may affect radically *Schools for the Future*. These are just some of the changes of the recent past:

- the advent of the new learning technologies
- consumer choice and its implications for schools
- a redefinition of the nature of schools in the education process
- the changing place of Britain in the global economy and in the development of global markets
- concerns about environmental issues and the use of resources
- revaluation of the place of non-teaching staff in the education process
- the pressure to achieve 'more for the same' brought about by budgetary constraints and increased emphasis on targets and performance measures.

So how should schools be responding to these challenges, and what can be done to support them?

School responses

Schools are already exploring solutions for a changing world. Some of these approaches can be broadly categorised as follows:

Increasing the emphasis on learning

Traditionally, the world of education has concentrated on teaching, making the assumption that learning will follow inevitably. However, the emphasis of the late 1980s and the 1990s on assessing and recording standards of achievement has forced a re-thinking of this simplistic view. Students' learning rather than teachers' teaching is increasingly seen to be at the crux of the education process: the emphasis has moved from inputs to outcomes.

Re-aligning teachers to be 'directors of learning'

The increasing emphasis on the process of learning has caused many schools, and teachers themselves, to review the teaching function. Teachers often now conceptualise their roles more in terms of 'directors of learning' than as purveyors of teaching. The change is a subtle one which does not deny the traditional 'art and science' of teaching; but it concentrates more on the use of those skills to bring about learning in the student.

Assessing the implications of the new technologies

Among the most powerful resources which teachers, as directors of learning, have at their disposal is the developing technology bound up in Information Technology. This opens up entirely new avenues of communication, making access to data simple, self-study a powerful tool, and availability of information international.

Extending teachers' roles to be managers of the learning environment in its widest sense

Old-fashioned concepts of 'one teacher, one class' for primary schools, or of 'one subject specialist, one class' in the secondary sector are, in the scenario we have painted, as redundant in the twenty-first century as Victorian pupil-monitors are today. The teachers of the future may exercise less of a role in class control or in the traditional skills of exposition: they may well be the programme-makers and resource creators of the future. They will not 'do the teaching', they will manage (in every sense) the intellectual environment that students will inhabit.

Reappraising patterns of learning

One of the implications of the picture painted here is that not only will teachers' roles and patterns of working change, but so will those of the learners. With more and more computers home-based, even portable, not all learning will need to take place in schools as they are currently modelled. The purposes of school buildings and their patterns of use will become subject to reappraisal.

What must we do?

Education stands at a cross-roads. One of the ways in which some educationists are dealing with this is to establish projects, such as the *Schools for the Future* project with which I have been involved at the University of Lincolnshire and Humberside. The project is primarily intended to support developments and changes for this twenty-first century world. It is attempting to do this in a number of ways, as shown below.

Through an analysis of change as it affects education

The project will be alert for, and seek out, the global and national trends in education which are likely to affect schools and learning in the immediate future.

Through research into innovative practice

In particular, the project will seek out innovative practice, large- or small-scale, in Britain and overseas. Whenever possible, we will try to explore at first hand not just the problems and their solutions, but the decision-making processes and creative approaches which have been used.

Through a specific research project on the use of school time and plant

The project team is already involved with a Funding Agency project in a group of schools in London. Here we are experimenting with one of the fundamental issues to face *Schools for the Future*: the structure of the school day and the school year. This is a collaborative venture located in three schools in which we shall be monitoring and evaluating not only the outcomes (in terms of new patterns of attendance and their effects), but also the kinds of radical thinking which are used to arrive at solutions.

Through an examination of the developing uses of new technologies in schools

One of the keys to future developments in education will, inevitably, be the uses to which new technologies are put. These are already developing as a powerful tool for communication, and to a lesser extent for learning. These parallel developments are set to continue; and the ways in which they are adopted into, and woven into the fabric of, educational provision in the future are potentially very challenging to traditional thinking about schools and their functions. The project will seek to explore both innovation in this field, and to speculate about alternative models of learning.

Through an examination of the decision-making processes and mind-sets needed to bring about dramatic change

This project is about dramatic, rather than marginal, change. In the project's studies of innovative practice we shall be as concerned with the thinking process leading to change as with the change itself. These are largely uncharted waters, and we shall be breaking new ground in exploring this issue – which may have implications for the selection and education of leaders for the future.

Through dissemination of best practice

A fundamental purpose of this project will be to pass on to the education world the lessons which we are able to learn. We shall do this through whatever channels are most appropriate: visits, courses, conferences, books, journal articles, in-service training events, the Internet and the media. Our main concern will not be to provide examples of practice which others may copy directly in their own situations, but to tease out the principles which others may apply to reach their own conclusions in their unique situations.

What are the broad philosophies behind the project?

Schools for the Future is based on the principles of reengineering. Michael Hammer defines reengineering as:

> *The fundamental rethinking and radical redesign of business processes to bring about dramatic improvements in performance"*
> *(Hammer, M and Champy, P (1997)* **The Reengineering Revolution Handbook.** *New York: Harper Business, p3).*

At the heart of the reengineering philosophy is the client/customer. Reengineering is about providing a better service in a changing environment; but it is more than tinkering with structures to achieve marginally more acceptable results. Reengineering uses the best insights from other management theories (team-work, total quality management, etc.), but is much more than the sum of these parts. It is a mind-set that uses creative thinking in a focused way to achieve quite different ways of working. It is anticipatory rather than reactive.

Reengineering and teaching skills

This series of books of teaching skills has developed out of my interest in reengineering as well as from my long-term involvement with the initial and in-service training of teachers. Part of the intention of the series is to identify those traditional teaching skills which will continue to be fundamental to the teacher in the twenty-first century, and to provide a means of support for those who wish to acquire or improve them. Thus class management is likely to remain a fundamental skill for teachers: but its nature will change to accommodate the new roles for teachers as directors of learning and as managers of para-professionals in the classroom. However, other skills, such as the exploitation of the new technologies, are of recent origin and will have to be assimilated by all teachers, including those who perhaps trained for a school system which operated rather differently in the recent past.

Education is changing rapidly; and the nature of the teacher's job is changing, too. Some people find change only negative and disturbing. This series treats change as a positive phenomenon: one which challenges and excites. Hopefully, these books do not lose sight of traditional wisdom nor of the continuing values of which the profession is rightly proud. But they do look forward in a spirit of progression and development to where schools are going rather than to where they have been.

Professor Trevor Kerry
Series Editor

How to use this book

This book aims to equip both beginning and more experienced teachers with the skills they need to become and remain effective classroom managers. For convenience of use the book is divided into seven chapters: starting with Basic Principles, moving through Rules and Relationships toward Other Things, before concluding with Child Protection.

The text is designed to present the essential knowledge about the skills of effective classroom management, in a style and language which is immediately accessible. Because the book consists of advice, guidance, ideas, strategies and tips, each discrete page has a major heading so that the educational issue is clearly presented then supported by an illustrative quotation. The text has been kept uncluttered. There are neither references to research nor further reading.

This book is designed to take the reader on from basic strategies for classroom control, to the subtleties of working with colleagues, by providing reliable routines through which the components of effective classroom management can be practised. It is suggested that readers make use of these routines and analyse their teaching to become reflective practitioners.

In practice, the book can be used in different ways:

■ It can be read as a continuous text: readers then adopt those routines which seem appropriate

■ It can be used as a training manual: readers incorporate each routine into their teaching

■ It can be used as a source book: the reader may dip into those sections which seem most pertinent at the time.

Similarly, the contexts of use may vary. The book can be used by an individual teacher working alone towards self-development. It can be used within a school, and the routines built into in-house professional development. The book could also form the basis for school-based in-service work led by an adviser, consultant, or facilitator. The material lends itself to use during teaching practices by initial trainees, or to reinforce skills during the early years of teaching. It may assist headteachers and other responsible for professional development to suggest a more focused way of improving classroom management.

Introduction

Education as the practice of freedom – as opposed to education as the practice of domination – denies that man is abstract, isolated, independent, and unattached to the world; it also denies that the world exists as a reality apart from men. Authentic reflection considers neither abstract man nor world without men, but men in their relations with the world.

(Paulo Freire, Pedagogy of the Oppressed)

This is a book about being in control. It is not for the control freak. It is not about the reactive, sterile control which creates passive pupils. It is not about Mr Shoutalot, doyen of the Wackford Squeers tendency, for whom no problem is so subtle that domination, rigidity and volume cannot produce a solution. This book is for the student teacher, the newly qualified teacher and the experienced practitioner. It is for those colleagues who wish to learn how to acquire and apply, or sharpen, successful classroom management strategies and techniques.

Effective teaching and learning cannot take place unless a teacher is in control and is managing events in the classroom. The control of the effective classroom manager is the control of the choreographer. They know where their pupils need to go to produce a high level of individual and group performance, and the steps he must lead them through to get there.

The effective classroom manager wants to know: what is it that I am doing well? What could I do better? Once you have answered these questions, you can decide whether any of the advice, guidance, ideas, strategies and tips offered in this book could help you to improve your classroom management.

I would like to acknowledge the following: Boroughbridge High School; Campsmount School, Norton, Doncaster; Dixons City Technology College, Bradford; Intake Primary School, Doncaster; Kelvin Hall High School, Kingston upon Hull; Malet Lambert High School, Kingston upon Hull; North Ferriby C of E Primary School; Oaklands School, York; Roscow Fold Primary School, Bolton; Thorpe Hesley Infant School, Rotherham and William Gee School, Kingston upon Hull.

John Bryson
www.educare.co.uk

Chapter 1

Basic principles

Success is a science; if you have the conditions, you get the results
(Oscar Wilde)

Your mission, as a teacher, is to both satisfy and delight your pupils. If they are to get some satisfaction and leave your lessons delighted, they will need to experience pleasure, joy and fulfilment. You will need to be their animator and facilitator.

As a classroom animator your task will be to provide interesting and lively lessons. As a facilitator you will make it easier for pupils to learn in those lessons. You will manage your classroom effectively because: 'Class management is what teachers do to ensure that children engage in the task in hand, whatever that may be' (Wragg, 1993).

Being an effective classroom manager is about being yourself, developing your own style. You will need to be yourself – with attitude. An attitude which

- expresses authority
- conveys enthusiasm

The techniques that create the conditions through which your Head of Department or Curriculum Co-ordinator ensure that children are on task and moving forward may be ineffective for you. 'There are many different ways of achieving the state where children work at the task in hand' (Wragg, 1993). Every effective classroom manager has to discover their way of achieving this state. They will need to discover their own way of making things happen in the classroom.

They will consolidate their successes and reshape their failures, by asking

- What have I done?
- What am I not doing?
- What else could I do?

Good teachers often break the rules. They may talk provocatively, or they may act outlandishly to make things happen. Whatever they do, to express their authority and convey enthusiasm, combines with their skillful management of pupils, resources and time to create successful learning opportunities. Their success comes from being themselves, not from being clones.

Effective classroom managers create the conditions to get the results they and their pupils desire by being aware of what they want to achieve. Effective classroom managers are proactive. Effective classroom managers are self evaluative. Effective classroom managers must be reflective practitioners.

Effective classroom management is based on these basic principles:

- expressing authority
- conveying enthusiasm
- proactivity
- preparation

Expressing authority

Teachers and pupils bring different constructions of reality to their shared experience of the classroom. These different constructions can be a source of conflict.

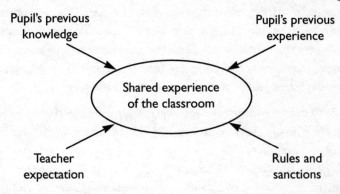

Figure 1.1 – *The construction of a classroom reality*

Control of this conflict is an important part of a teacher's job. For many teachers, and other members of the wider school community, reduction of this conflict and good classroom control means order, regularity and passivity – an unholy trinity which does not work in the best interests of pupils.

Most pupils recognise that teachers have authority. They know that teachers can use a set of rules and sanctions to achieve their aims. They may also see the classroom as a place in which the teacher is tested as they bargain with them for control.

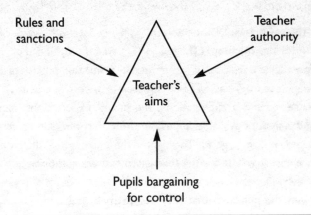

Figure 1.2 – *Don't you just love being in control?*

The effective classroom manager will pass this test. They will strike a bargain which benefits all the pupils. They will use their skills to create a learning environment in which all partners to the classroom contract – parents, pupils, governors, senior management and colleagues – understand the need for appropriate forms of behaviour.

The ineffective classroom manager will fail this test. The classroom will be a place where rules, sanctions and the behaviour of the teacher and/or pupils no longer support their aims. Their failure to maintain good order and school discipline will deny the pupils the opportunity to learn. They will deny themselves professional fulfilment and job satisfaction.

The purpose of classroom control is not the exercise of authority for its own sake, but the facilitation of learning. Positive, proactive control provides pupils with opportunities to learn and develop their abilities.

An important consideration for the effective classroom manager, when expressing authority, will be to use less external discipline and control. Pupils should be encouraged to accept responsibility for their own actions and share in decision making.

The class teacher will need to use their personal and professional authority to draw together different constructions of classroom reality and make them work the way they want them to.

When they use their authority, they will need to be aware of 'the definition of the situation' (Thomas, 1931) which they and their pupils will have. This definition is constructed from the pupils' previous knowledge (see Figure 1.1: *The Construction of a Classroom Reality*), their experience, teacher's expectations, the pupils' expectations, plus the rules and sanctions available for use in the classroom (see *Roscow Fold KS1 Classroom Plan*, page 6). The tighter the definition of the situation, the more easy it will be for the teacher to express authority. In a more loosely defined situation the teacher may need to 'negotiate' (Strauss, 1964) with the pupils so that they accept their authority. During this negotiation they can use both verbal and non-verbal signals.

Verbal signals	Non-verbal signals
Commands	Eye Contact
Conversation	Gestures
Questions	Position in the classroom
Responses	Posture/Body language
	Property rights
	Space and its invasion
	Territory
	Touching (be careful)

The big question about effective classroom management is: how does the newly qualified teacher acquire authority and how does the experienced teacher maintain authority?

According to Shirley Conran first, second and third impressions count. How the newly qualified teacher presents themselves to a class matters.

The effective classroom manager

Who walks in the classroom cool and slow?
(Jerry Leiber and Mike Stoller, Charlie Brown)

The effective classroom manager can begin to exercise the right kind of control by:

- Understanding their own behaviour.
- Realising that many classroom problems are a direct consequence of teacher behaviour.
- Never considering a pupil's behaviour in isolation.
- Reducing the impact of problems created by organisation and administration.

- Providing pupils with a model of the attitudes and behaviours expected of them.
- Showing pupils that you care about their work and their lives both inside and outside the school.
- Being consistent, fair and firm.
- Using teaching strategies which involve praise.
- Adopting a flexible approach when things are not working.
- Persevering with a positive, proactive approach to classroom management.

Key Stage 1 classroom plan

Dear Parents

At Roscow Fold we are keen to promote an atmosphere which gives every child guidance in making good decisions about her or his behaviour and thereby creates a positive environment which supports the learning process. We regard you as partners in your child's education, so I am writing to give you details of our Key Stage 1 (Reception-Year 2) classroom discipline plan and to ask you to support us in developing a structure of rules and rewards for appropriate behaviour and a set of consequences for inappropriate behaviour.

The Classroom Plan

Rules

1.   *Follow directions.*
2.   *Be kind to each other.*
3.   *Take care of everything.*
4.   *Ask permission before leaving the room.*

Rewards for appropriate behaviour
1   Praise.
2   Stickers and badges.
3   Certificates to take home.
4   Friday book.
5   Merit cup.
6   Sent to Headteacher.
7   Class and group awards.

Consequences for inappropriate behaviour
1   A warning.
2   'Time out' in class.
3   Last out for playtime.
4   Speak to parent.
5   Sent to Headteacher.

Please discuss this plan with your child. If you have any queries or comments about it, please do not hesitate to contact me.

Thank you for your co-operation.

Yours sincerely,

(Headteacher)

Conveying enthusiasm

An enthusiastic teacher shows their pupils that they care about their progress and welfare. Analyse the behaviour of effective classroom managers and you will see that they are effective because they care. Their pupils listen attentively because they are aware that their teacher is saying something important.

If you don't care, why should your pupils take any notice?

A teacher's authority rests, to a large extent, on consent. A consent which can be more easily acquired if the teacher promotes a cooperative atmosphere in the classroom. This does not mean that teachers should tolerate inappropriate behaviour to avoid confrontation. It means that teachers should show their pupils how to behave through positive role modelling.

An enthusiastic teacher will

- Be in the classroom before their pupils
- Control entry and welcome pupils into the classroom
- Start lessons energetically and promptly
- Make their objectives clear
- Provide an organised and orderly conclusion to lessons
- Demand cooperative on-task behaviour
- Exercise quiet, consistent, control at all times
- Avoid using sarcasm as a means of control
- Create light moments through humour
- Listen carefully when pupils are talking
- Praise pupils whenever possible
- Provide positive feedback for pupils

Such a positive model can contribute to a shared perception of roles and lead to a shared understanding of appropriate behaviour. An appropriate behaviour which is largely defined by previous experience and current expectations. The example on page 10 shows how all members of Campsmount School have an agreed understanding of appropriate behaviour and the consequences which automatically follow is a pupil chooses to behave inappropriately. An enthusiastic newly qualified teacher can build upon these established expectations to create a secure, sympathetic environment in their classroom.

Proactivity

Don't wait for things to happen, you will lose the initiative and be unable to achieve your aims and objectives. Pupils' attention can be improved and sustained by

- Standing in a prominent position in the classroom
- Patrolling, moving close to inattentive pupils
- Making and maintaining eye contact with individual pupils
- Encouraging feedback from pupils

Preparation

Preparation is concerned with being ready to satisfy and delight pupils and includes:

- Planning schemes of work and lesson to ensure continuity
- Preparing differentiated work which is appropriate to the age and ability of pupils
- Providing tasks which intellectually challenge pupils
- Creating an appropriate classroom layout and seating plans

Well prepared lessons have clear aims and objectives. The effective classroom manager expects specific results. There is often more than one objective. They have an overall one which is the aim of the lesson, such as to explain a fresh concept or to lead pupils through a particular process. Also, within the lesson there may be many different objectives:

- Motivating less committed pupils
- Consolidating previous learning
- Making pupils pleased with their performance
- Establishing credibility as a teacher
- Reducing tensions and helping pupils to relax by making them laugh

If you combine these basic principles with some of the strategies which follow, you will be able to create your own system of effective classroom management which minimises disruption and maximises efficiency.

Remember, don't smile until Christmas. The greatest equation of the twentieth century may not be Einstein's $E = MC^2$. It could be $ER + P = C$. That is, Early Relaxation + Pupils = Chaos.

All members of Campsmount School

Accept Challenges
Value Achievement
Respect Others

Pupil rules

1 All pupils to be ready and working five minutes after start of lesson (second bell will sound).

2 All pupils should be fully equipped for all lessons with pen, pencil and ruler.

3 All pupils will raise their hands to attract teachers' attention – **they must not call out**.

4 All pupils will remain seated unless given permission to move.

5 All pupils will treat staff, fellow pupils and the school with care and respect.

YOU HAVE THE CHOICE!

PROPOSED SANCTIONS

i Name put on board
ii Five minute detention at next available break
iii Ten minute detention at next available break
iv Thirty minute detention at lunchtime
v One hour detention after school
vi Isolation from lessons until parents contact school
vii Exclusion

PROPOSED REWARDS

One point awarded for each good lesson, then at end of each term:

400 points = Bronze award – min time 1 term

800 points = Silver award – min time 2 terms

1200 points = Gold award – min time 3 terms

Awards must run consecutively

Basic principles checklist

- Being an effective classroom manager is all about being yourself.
- Effective classroom managers are reflective practitioners. They evaluate their own performance by asking:

    What have I done?

    What am I not doing?

    What else could I do?

- You are responsible for expressing authority.
- Make sure that all partners to your classroom contract understand what is appropriate behaviour.
- Make sure that the structure of rules and rewards is known to everyone.
- The purpose of control is the facilitation of learning.
- Don't blame your pupils for your mistakes.
- Know where your pupils are, where they need to go, and the steps they must take to get there.
- Manage all resources carefully.
- Enthusiasm can be contagious.

Desk top tool kit

Man is a tool using animal
(Carlyle, Sartor Resartus)

You will need to keep the following items (permanently marked with your name) in a safe accessible place:

- ball point pens
- felt tip pens (non-permanent)
- overhead projector pens
- HB pencils
- two quality pencil sharpeners
- coloured pencils
- a shatterproof ruler
- sharp scissors (for your own use)
- a non-toxic glue stick
- sellotape
- blu-tac
- a stapler, staples and staple remover
- drawing pins
- dressmaking pins with coloured heads
- paperclips
- bulldog clips
- elastic bands
- non-toxic correction fluid
- a solar powered calculator
- post-it notes
- smiley face stickers
- blank recording cassettes
- paper tissues
- chalk/white board cleaner
- white and coloured chalk
- board pens

Cupboard tool kit

Without tools he is nothing
(Carlyle, Sartor Resartus)

You will need to keep the following items (permanently marked with your name) in a safe, lockable place; marked not for use by pupils.

- a stanley knife
- standard and crossdrive screwdrivers
- a claw hammer
- a pin hammer
- an assortment of nails
- an assortment of standard and crossdrive screws
- superglue
- superglue remover
- a glue gun
- numbered cards
- a pack of sewing needles
- an assortment of sewing threads
- a heavy duty hole puncher
- a timer
- ten paracetamol tablets (for personal use)
- throat pastilles (for personal use)
- bottled water (for personal use)
- a small first aid kit (for personal use)
- fresh wipes (for personal use)
- hand lotion (for personal use)
- a whistle
- birthday candles

- matches (for lighting birthday candles)
- a variety of plastic and carrier bags
- a dustpan and brush
- a torch and batteries

Essential equipment

... with tools he is all
(Carlyle, Sartor Resartus)

You will need to know where the following items are kept and how to book them for use in your classroom:

- an overhead projector on a trolley (it is better to have a wall mounted screen or a piece of white wall rather than a free-standing screen)
- spare overhead projector bulbs (learn how to replace them)
- a tape recorder, microphones and headphones
- a camera (preferably Polaroid) and film
- a computer on a trolley - if one is not dedicated to your classroom
- a video player and television (unless there is a dedicated viewing area)
- extra tables and chairs

The construction of a classroom reality

Human kind cannot bear very much reality

(T.S. Eliot)

Although classroom behaviour may appear to be pre-mapped by codes such as those employed at Campsmount and Roscow Fold, and be founded upon rules and principles, there will be grey areas where the rules are not clear or where there is insufficient agreement about the rules and the force with which they should be applied. This emphasises the problematical nature of the classroom and takes us back to the big question: how does the newly qualified teacher acquire authority and how does the experienced teacher maintain their authority?

When an NQT meets their class for the first time they have to remember Shirley Conran's maxim that first, second and third impressions count. Both they and their class will be faced with many possible courses of action. Together, they will need to find a consistently meaningful path to follow. The NQT will have to take decisions and make judgements which will commit them to particular lines of action.

The interaction in the NQT's classroom will be a meeting of different constructions of reality. By effectively managing the negotiation which will take place, as their pupils try to establish what is happening in the classroom and try to influence outcomes, the NQT will begin to acquire personal authority.

The kind of negotiation which takes place will be influenced by the previous knowledge of the interactants, and by their relative status. It may be easier for Mr or Mrs Shoutalot to establish a quiet, *working* atmosphere because they already have an established reputation for being *hard*. The NQT, an unknown entity, will be appraised and tested by the pupils as they bargain for control.

This bargaining may take place in a variety of ways. For instance, pupils will expect the teacher to be consistent and to be more or less in line with other teachers. Therefore, the first offer in the negotiating process is vital.

Meeting classes for the first time

Go ahead, make my day
(Clint Eastwood as Dirty Harry*)*

- Don't smile until Christmas: once pupils decide you are a soft touch there is no second chance.
- Write your name on the blackboard and introduce yourself.
- Establish some simple rules.
- Invite pupils to draw up a class code of conduct – ownership is vital.
- Learn names quickly.
- Encourage pupils to introduce each other to the class.
- Outline the first half term's work – link it to the National Curriculum Programmes of Study and examination board syllabus.
- Outline the methods of assessment which will be used.
- Find out what pupils already know.
- Explain which resources are for pupils' use and where they are kept.
- Be vigilant – react rapidly if rules are broken.
- Name names when things go wrong.

Getting and holding attention

Ground control to Major Tom
(David Bowie, Space Oddity, 1969)

School children of all ages are lively and animated, and you will want them to be enthusiastic and ready to learn. Pick and mix from the following suggestions to suit your style.

- When pupils are waiting outside the classroom use the opportunity to tell them how to enter.
- Welcome pupils into the classroom – make them aware that it is your classroom. Tell them what to do.
- Stand still and silent until they notice you, then tell them what to do.
- Do not shout. Noisy teachers make noisy pupils.
- Make eye contact with someone, put a finger to your lips and say 'ssh'. Train pupils to pass it on.
- Develop strategies to encourage a quiet start to your lesson. For example, ten minutes USSR – Uninterrupted Sustained Silent Reading.
- Praise pupils who are listening. Praise works better than nagging noisy members of a class.
- Do not have any unproductive time at the beginning of a lesson, train pupils to begin work as soon as they arrive in your classroom.
- Use the 'Casablanca Syndrome'. Round up the usual suspects and give them specific tasks.

Handling interruptions

The trouble with Freud is that he never played the Glasgow
Empire Saturday night
(Ken Dodd)

- Never ignore an interruption.

- Stop what you are doing. Make a note of where you have stopped,

- Is the interruption necessary? If so be kind to the pupil who has interrupted you.

- Do not lose your rag with time-wasting colleagues. Speak to them later.

- Try to turn a negative interruption into something positive and demonstrate to pupils that you welcome their involvement in lessons.

- Have Plan 'B' ready for interruptions. All the best ad libs are well planned. A short list of relevant questions can help to draw a heckler's fire.

- Be a space invader. Intimidate hecklers by moving close to them.

- Look for causes. Why do regular hecklers adopt this pattern of behaviour?

- Share ideas with colleagues at an INSET workshop?

Learning names

Allow their names to be mentioned
(Jane Austen, Pride and Prejudice)

Naming names is vital for effective classroom management.

- Some pupils do not like their given names. Within reason, allow pupils to decide their own names.

- Make sure that you are using correct names. Check pronunciation of unfamiliar names.

- Remember, familiarity breeds contempt. You are the class teacher, not their mate. Avoid using nicknames.

- Begin a new class/term/year with name badges or desktop name plates. Reinforce the use of this by examples – conferences for instance.

- Make a seating plan and insist that pupils sit in their allocated place.

- Use your seating plan, or class register, to select pupils by name to answer questions.

- Always use a pupil's name. Reinforce the fact that you know them as individuals.

- First names first, then pick up the surnames later.

- How many Darrens do you have? Differentiate.

- Return exercise books by name – link the person with the name.

Seating arrangements

In the third-class seat sat the journeying boy
(Thomas Hardy, Midnight on the Great Western)

Left to their own devices pupils will normally choose to sit with their best friends, their friend of the moment, in peer groups or in isolation – none of which is the best arrangement for learning.

- Younger pupils need to be seated in patterns that are conducive to learning.
- Ensure that pupils with hearing or vision problems sit where they can see the board and hear what you say.
- Ensure that chairs and desks do not obstruct pathways or create health and safety risks.
- When arranging discussion groups ensure that pupils with hearing difficulties are carefully seated.
- Place known isolates in supportive groups.
- It is a good idea to allocate seats for the first half term of an academic year to establish your authority – pupils who cooperate can then choose their own seats.
- Seating arrangements for older pupils can be more flexible. On occasions allow them to choose their own work groups.
- Elect a seating sub-committee to draw up a class seating plan – retain the right of veto, or act as a consultant.
- When pupils are comfortable with each other try allocating seats by drawing numbers.
- Use squared paper to design a classroom layout to suit the needs of your class.
- Consider angles of vision when planning a classroom layout – place your desk in a corner where you have a better view.

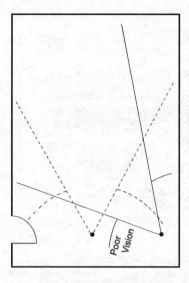

Figure 1.3 – A corner position gives a better field of view

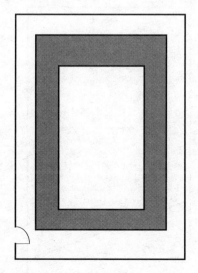

Figure 1.4 – Possible Seating Arrangements 1
A boardroom layout is best for large group discussions.

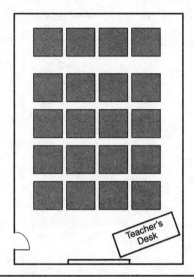

Figure 1.5 – *Possible Seating Arrangements 2*
A theatre layout is best for whole class lessons and presentations

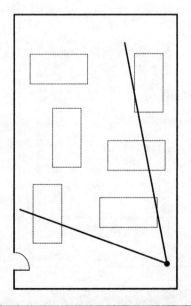

Figure 1.6 – *Possible Seating Arrangements 3*
A work station layout is best for small group tasks

Writing on boards

How can you contrive to write so even?
(Jane Austen, Pride and Prejudice)

There should be a chalkboard or whiteboard in every teaching space. Learn to use both.

- Can they read it at the back? Check that your writing is readable from the back of the room.
- Start at the top. The bottom of the board may not be visible further back in the room.
- Use your board as an aide memoire when asking questions. Add answers as the lesson progresses.
- Do not talk to the board. Speak to the class, then write on the board.
- Do not limit your field of view.
- If possible, prepare your board before a lesson.
- Ask pupils to write on the board and own their contribution to a lesson.
- Reinforce the value of pupils' work before you clean the board.
- Do not use permanent marker pens on a whiteboard.
- If others use your room, always leave a clean board.

Practical lessons

Prepared for either event
(Virgil, Aeneid)

There is no point in turning a drama into a crisis, so never attempt anything new with a class until you have tried it out and know that it works.

- Have you got everything you need?
- Is everything ready to go?
- Keep materials in labelled boxes for another time.
- Involve pupils when it is safe to do so. They can give things out and collect them in at the end of the lesson.
- Keep instructions systematic and clear. Draw poor listeners in with questions.
- Make demonstrations sharp and well focused.
- Build on the code of conduct – health and safety is vital at all times.
- Encourage pupils to help each other.
- Pupils will need to work at their own pace – so stop, recap and move on at intervals during the lesson.
- Bring the lesson to a conclusion with an evaluation of what has been achieved – pupils can show and tell.

Equal opportunities

We hold these truths to be sacred and undeniable; that all men are created equal and independent
(Thomas Jefferson, The American Declaration of Independence*)*

All pupils should be treated and valued equally.

- Ask boys and girls equal numbers of questions.
- Arrange mixed-gender work groups.
- Learn to pronounce unfamiliar names.
- Avoid allocating roles according to race, gender, sexuality, age or disability.
- Ask boys and girls to do the same jobs.
- Politely draw colleagues' attention to any violations of equal opportunity principles and policies.
- Watch you language.
- Do not make fun of pupils – laugh with them.
- Encourage pupils to confront inequality and find solutions to evident problems.
- Be a good role model. Let pupils see you working with colleagues of different race, gender, sexuality, age and ability.
- Help pupils who act in a biased way to appreciate the importance of equality.

Giving feedback

Whatsoever things are true... think on these things
(Philippians, 4:8)

- Receiving feedback, especially in public, can be a difficult experience.
- When returning exercise books to a whole class only make positive, supportive comments.
- Positive body language, facial expression and tone of voice should be used to emphasise your message.
- Reinforce face-to-face feedback with written comments on which pupils can reflect.
- Ask questions to ensure that a pupil is receiving the message you want to deliver.
- Give general information to a whole class.
- Give specific information to individuals as privately as possible.
- Prepare a short script to ensure that you do not miss out any vital points.
- Start and finish your feedback with something your pupil will want to hear.
- Change your approach if a pupil is upset.
- Allow pupils an opportunity to tell you what they think and feel about their learning.

Gathering feedback

People ask you for criticism, but they only want praise
(W. Somerset Maugham, Of Human Bondage)

- Feedback from pupils helps you to be reflective. Analyse their body language, expressions and responses for information.

- Encourage pupils to think about what is happening in your classroom and support their feedback to you.

- Collect individual feedback when you are discussing a pupil's work with her.

- Turn problems into solutions by encouraging pupils to explain why they think a difficulty has arisen.

- Use focus groups, individuals, evaluation sheets and questionnaires to gather feedback on particular activities or issues.

- Do not be falsely modest – accept feedback which praises your performance.

- Always accept negative feedback in a positive way: listen and consider it carefully before you respond.

- Ensure that your pupils can see that you value their feedback to you.

- Create a positive culture in your classroom. There is no criticism – only feedback.

Chapter 2

Planning and assessment

Target setting

There are two things to aim at in life: first, to get what you want; and after that, to enjoy it
(Logan Pearsall Smith, Afterthoughts)

- Identify your target.
- What do you want to achieve?
- Outline each target, in writing, on one side of A4 paper.
- What do you need to know to attain your target?
- Who or what do you need to help you?
- Who needs to know about this target?
- Agree performance indicators to inform your evaluation of your performance.

- Agree a time span for attaining your target and any intermediate aims.
- Regularly review your progress.
- What is your next target?

Individual Education Plan

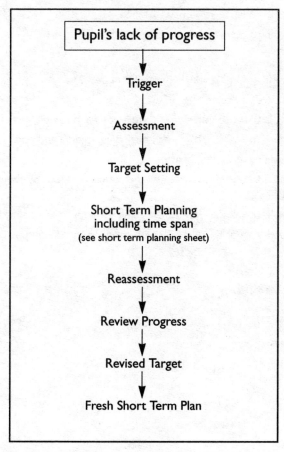

This process can be helpful in identifying a pupil's need and creating a quality assured whole school approach to target setting.

Triggers

Concerns arising from pupils' lack of progress can be labelled and tabulated as triggers to make identifying needs a simplified formal process.

Year 1 (during half term)

- Unable to recognise 10 key words
- Unable to recognise 10 sounds
- Unable to write without assistance
- Unable to read, write or order numbers from 1 to 10

Year 5

- Attainment at National Curriculum Level 2
- Standardised tests
- Unable to write one side with full stops and capital letters
- Unable to write a story with beginning, middle and end
- Unable to use a dictionary
- Unable to attempt written mathematical problems without assistance
- Unable to tell the time to five minutes from an analogue clock
- Unable to work within 100 with carrying and decomposition

Recording Special Needs

A framework for identifying and recording a pupil's special needs

Class teachers are responsible for identifying those pupils in their class who fail to make normal progress

↓

Class teacher makes an initial assessment of the pupil's needs and provides differentiated work

↓

Class teacher closely monitors and reviews progress, keeping pieces of work as a record of work covered

↓

Class teacher consults SENCO who registers the pupil on the school's special needs register

↓

The pupil's parents are informed

School Expression of Concern

NAME	CLASS	DoB 00.00.00	SUBJECT	TEACHER	DATE 00.00.00
Concern	Evidence		Strategies used		Pupil Response/Outcome
Reading	Photocopied work		Discussion with parents		
Comprehension	Test Results		Discussion with pupil		
Spelling			Differentiation		
Handwriting			Extra time		
Number	**National Curriculum Levels**		Shorter answers		
	AT1 Level				
	AT2 Level		Individual Worksheets		
Other	AT3 Level				
	AT4 Level		Support Teacher		
			Pair Work		
	CAT Test				
	Verbal		Group Work		
	Quantitative				
	Non-Verbal		Individual attention		
	Mean				
			Other		

Concerns Sheet

> School
>
> √ **Learning Support**

From _____ Subject _____

Name	Form	7	8	9	10	11

Nature of Concern
(Please be specific as possible – see over)

Is this pupil receiving any support to your knowledge?

Please comment on any action/strategies you have already tried and to what effect:

Type of support sought

- Please enclose a typical sample of the pupil's work where appropriate.
- You may wish to use the following as a checklist:

Reading skills
- mechanical
- comprehension
- researching

Spelling and technical writing skills – handwriting, punctuation etc.

Written expression

Communication skills
- listening
- speaking
- giving and receiving instructions

Perceptual and motor skills

Co-ordination

Mathematics

Self-confidence

Concentration

Please return to AB, thank you

Target writing

1 Targets are carefully defined developmental steps, easily understood by any adult or teacher working with a pupil.

2 Targets should be directly related to the skills that a pupil is expected to achieve in a given time. They should be:
   - specific
   - clear
   - achievable

3 Use a verb to describe the target that a pupil is expected to achieve:
   - to write
   - to know
   - to recognise

4 Steps should be clear, cumulative, factual and informative.

5 The target should be clearly related to a specific time – by the next progress review, the pupil will know...

6 The record of targets should provide detailed information about progress made over a given period of time.

7 The record of targets should provide a comprehensive picture of a pupil's achievement.

8 Targets are an integral part of the teaching and learning process – they should be linked to NC Programmes of Study whenever possible.

9 Ability specific, age appropriate targets incorporate the assessment process into day-to-day teaching and learning.

10 Targets should be directly linked to skills and/or emotional and/or social development.

11 Targets should provide information about a pupils development.

12 Examples of a pupil's work should demonstrate attainment.

13 Working on the Dorcan Scheme is not a target, as it describes the use of a specific resource. It does not describe the specific skills a pupil is to achieve.

14 A target should be clearly defined:
- to be able to construct a sentence using words from Set 1;
- to be able to spell from dictation using words from Set 2;
- to be able to write a sentence using words from Set 3.

15 Targets can be generated using schemes such as:
- SNIPP
  National Curriculum Maths and English
  Northumberland County Council
- Profiles of Development
  National Curriculum Maths, English and Science
  Avec Designs Limited
- Portage Checklist
  NFER
- Early Years Easy Screen (EYES) for younger children
  NFER.

Hightown Grammar School IEP

Individual Education Plan Stage 2

Name: **Class:**   **Date:**

Summary of difficulties

Areas of weakness – rapid recall of basic number bonds. Tables from 2x. Concept of basic multiplication needs reinforcing. Fractions, spatial tasks, finds symbols confusing. Setting out of work clearly and tens and units need attention.

Test results: Youngs Maths

                    Year 7 module test I

                    Year 7 module test 2

SEN Provision: Support and small group work

Targets:
- To revisit and reinforce basic fractions.
- To learn 2 and 3 times tables.
- To perform simple practical operations to reinforce concept of +.
- To read a simple decimal scale.
- To read a simple scale of negative values.

Next Review:

Team action target*

TARGET: (What do we need to achieve?)				
STRATEGIES, RESOURCES NEEDED: (What do we need to do?) (Who/what do we need to help us?)				
PERFORMANCE INDICATORS or SUCCESS CRITERIA: (How will we know when we have fulfilled our target?)				
TIME SPAN (How long will we allow to achieve this?)				
AGREED RECIPIENT for this particular target: (Who needs to know about this target?)				

*From an idea in use at Boroughbridge High School, North Yorkshire

Differentiation

Everybody is ignorant, only on different subjects
(New York Times. 31 August 1924)

'The purpose of education for all children is the same; the goals are the same. But the help that individual children need in progressing towards them will be different' (Warnock, 1978). The National Curriculum has changed Warnock's goals into Attainment Targets – the impetus for differentiation. Differentiation doesn't just happen. It is planned intervention in the learning process to make a difference. Differentiation is concerned with the planning effective classroom managers do (see *short term planning*, page 44).

Simplistic organisational responses to these demands of the National Curriculum cannot meet the needs of differences in the abilities and characteristics of pupils. In any class, whether settled or mixed ability, there will be wide variation in:

- listening skills
- presentation skills
- ability to be cooperative
- ability to work independently
- the amount and quality of homework pupils can do
- the amount and quality of work pupils complete in a lesson

The complex web of pupils' needs, characteristics and abilities demands a more sophisticated response. The effective classroom manager is, therefore, working on a response which tackles the big questions. How can teaching and learning styles move a pupil from where she is now to where she has the potential to be? How can lesson planning accommodate pupils' different preferred ways of moving from where they are now to where they have the potential to be? The answers to these big questions include a readiness to accept that the National Curriculum can help teachers to intervene in the learning process to make a difference:

- through assessment of what individual pupils know, understand and can do
- by using these assessments and programmes of study to describe the needs of individual pupils
- by planning learning experiences based on a pupil's achievements.

Intervention to ensure that pupils maximise their potential shouldn't happen just once. It is a continuous process, involving assessment to recognise individual needs within a class, planning to meet these needs, appropriate teaching and learning strategies and an evaluation of the process. This places differentiation firmly in the classroom. The model below shows how it can work.

Content –	defined by statute
Outcomes –	vary according to ability +
Differentiated	
Response	from teachers and peers
Resources	appropriate to the task
Support	to help and guide
Tasks	designed to enable pupils

Differentiated response

Pupils with unique combinations of strengths and weaknesses, working on a common set of tasks, will produce very different finished or incomplete products. These differentiated outcomes demand different responses. The following strategies can be used to develop differentiated responses.

- Learning logs allow teachers and pupils to comment on the process of learning and the quality of the product. Pupils can be encouraged to think about their thinking, and learn about their learning. At the end of a lesson pupils are allowed quiet time to record their impressions of the lesson – becoming reflective learners.

- Pair and small group tutoring provides more individual support than class teaching.
- Assessment criteria should be clearly linked to the abilities, interests and needs of individual pupils.
- Match response to achievement – to be effective feedback should relate to a pupil's past achievement rather than abstract criteria.
- Individual Action Plans (see *target setting*) incorporate a differentiated response into plans for the future.
- Explaining learning objectives in accessible language enables pupils to link the teacher's response to the task they have completed.
- Response partners can comment on each other's work. Many English teachers encourage pupils to write on one side of a double page to allow space for comments (see *self and peer assessment*).

Differentiated resources

Your school will have appropriate resources to enable pupils to learn the content of your phase or subject area. Pupils may already follow individual proprietary programmes supplemented by in-house resources.

Both types of resources can be used to enable differentiation to take place. You can select specific items for particular purposes:

1 Ease of use:
   - clear, explained sequencing of tasks
   - left justified printing to provide vital clues to the next line of text
   - selection of language appropriate for the age group
2 Safe and suitable design:
   - provision of appropriate examples
   - visual images to improve appeal
   - appropriate illustrations to break up passages of text.
3 Readability levels can be tested through a variety of software.
4 As pupils differ in the way they make use of resources the effective classroom manager needs to provide a wide variety of media and other resources to capitalise on these differences.

5 Technology can be used to make information more accessible:

- interactive CD-ROMs enable pupils to respond to a stimulus without writing
- Concept Keyboards enable pupils to create sentences in a target language which can then be printed out for them
- tape recordings of key learning can make written text more accessible

Differentiated support

Some pupils need more help than others. When we give them assistance, we are providing differentiation by support – which needs to be systematic. Here are some helpful strategies:

- individual work with a teacher
- individual and small group work with a classroom assistant or an adult volunteer
- computer based learning packages such as interactive CD-ROMs
- small group tutoring which provides quality time and helps to avoid stigmatising the less able
- create an achievement culture by celebrating individual, group and whole class successes
- cooperate with colleagues to produce teaching materials which promote small group activities and allow classes to be combined to share resources.

Differentiated tasks

All pupils are unique. They bring different abilities, aptitudes and prior experiences into the classroom. They collect different sets of working styles. Effective classroom managers need to provide a range of differentiated tasks, that cover the knowledge and skills to be acquired by their pupils, to empower the variety of individuals in a class. The following strategies may be helpful.

I Design appropriate tasks offering different starting points – including variety in aptitude, experience, level, media, skills, styles and type.

2 Match tasks to pupils' abilities, aptitudes, interests and prior experience:
   - is the task open or closed?
   - provide different starting points
   - is the task core curriculum or extension?
   - provide opportunities for extension activities
   - include individual, pair and small group work
   - allow contributions to be independent of writing skills
   - provide for whole class discussion to share understanding
   - stimulus should allow discussions to progress at different levels of complexity.

3 Ensure that students stay on task by:
   - highlighting expectations
   - providing clear instructions
   - providing self assessment
   - providing timed progress checks.

4 Design tasks which allow a variety of outputs to demonstrate individual strengths.

5 Provide a range of tasks to allow pupils to choose:
   - provide opportunities to stretch individual pupils
   - allow some choice in the complexity of the activity
   - guide individuals towards the most suitable activities
   - include activities which allow pupils to define their own areas of investigation and ensure ownership.

6 Design learning routes which recognise different levels of ability:
   - provide different starting points
   - include ability-specific tasks
   - emphasise high expectations
   - include extension activities for the more able
   - include common tasks to allow for pair and small group tutoring.

Differentiation is planned by you

Planning schemes of work

The best laid schemes o' mice and men Gang aft a-gley
(*Robert Burns,* To a Mouse)

1 A good scheme of work is adaptable – plan in some flexibility (see *scheme for Friedrich*, page 45)

2 Learning outcomes are the basis of an effective plan. Identify skills and knowledge to be acquired by pupils (see *short term planning for It's not the end of the world*, page 44).

3 Clearly describe your teaching aims and objectives:

■ My pupils will...

4 Differentiate to allow all pupils to flourish.

5 Ensure that assessments are planned early and clearly linked to your teaching aims and objectives.

■ This will show that my pupils have ...

6 Use a variety of assessment opportunities to allow all pupils to demonstrate their capabilities.

7 Describe the evidence pupils will need to collect to show that they have achieved the learning outcomes.

8 Build in, do not bolt on, cross-curricular issues (see *Friedrich scheme*, page 45).

9 Collect the resources which you will require.

10 The first half of an academic year is usually the most productive – allocate time accordingly.

Short term planning

This Short Term Planning proforma allows effective classroom managers to describe:

- their learning objectives
- the activities which pupils will undertake to achieve these objectives
- the differentiation needed to provide equality of opportunity
- means of assessment
- fresh targets, and
- the required resources.

English Short Term Planning	Group	Date			
Learning Objectives	**Activities**		**Differentiation**	**Assessment**	**Targets**
■ to be able to read with appropriate expression	■ Etymology of COP		Teacher input 1 to 1		
■ to be able to read, deduce and infer	■ Discuss Jeff's disappearance and who will look for him				
■ to be able to plan and and improve their work	■ Spider plan				
■ to be able to retell what they have read, sequencing stages	■ Read chapter 24				
	■ Look critically at what Mom and Daddy say				
■ to be able to make notes during/after reading	■ Write Sgt Tice's monologue				
	■ Design a missing persons poster about Jeff				
■ to be able to draft and re-draft their work	■ Write Karen's next letter to Garfa based on chs 23 & 24				
Resources _It's not the end of the world_ Writing paper Mom/Daddy Analysis sheets Missing persons data sheet					

A good scheme of work is adaptable and flexible. These sample activities from a scheme for studying Hans Peter Richter's novel _Friedrich_ allow pupils of all abilities access to the text and provide exciting assessment opportunities.

Friedrich by Hans Peter Richter

Features

- A good class reader for 12 to 14-year-olds.
- An accessible, compelling narrative.
- A moving account of the persecution of the Jews in Nazi Germany.
- An ideal text for PSE/cross curricular lessons as it defines issues of tolerance and intolerance, justice and injustice.
- An eyewitness account of the rise of the Nazi party.

Aims

The aim of this scheme is to encourage an integrated programme of English, involving reading, writing, talking and listening. The unit will seek to develop pupils' ability to communicate orally and in writing their ideas, knowledge, feelings and points of view; to understand and respond appropriately to others; to read, enjoy and respond to literature in a wide variety of ways; to speak and write effectively and appropriately.

Before reading

1 Through research into the Treaty of Versailles and the Weimar Republic try to decide why Hitler and the Nazi party gained power in Germany.

2 Use the library and Encarta to find out about the General Strike and the Jarrow Marchers.

3 Use a spider plan to explore Justice and Injustice.

HOMEWORK – bring a newspaper cutting that you think shows an example of Justice or Injustice.

4 As a whole class discuss your ideas about Justice and Injustice and the newspaper cuttings which you have

collected. Display the cuttings and your spider plans to provide a visual definition of your views/ideas.

Write some graffiti to give your display a cutting edge (be careful).

5 Listen to Robin Archer singing Brecht songs.

6 Listen to Alan Price's 'Jarrow Song'.

7 Listen to some songs from *Cabaret* and watch extracts from the film (be careful).

During Reading

The text will be read in the following ways:

(a) teacher reading/pupils listening;

(b) pupil reading silently with sustained concentration (USSR);

(c) pupil reading aloud to a partner;

(d) pupil reading aloud as a member of a small group;

(e) pupil reading aloud to the whole class (volunteers only).

8 Read Setting the Scene and Potato Cakes.

In small groups talk about the characters.

9 As you read the story make a note of evidence of poverty and prosperity in the two families.

10 As you read the story collect information about each character.

Write police files for each character, with relevant details about their activities.

11 Write extracts from Friedrich's diary, about the narrator, Helga, and other significant characters in the story.

12 Read up to page 25. Prepare to write two letters with different tones.

Grandfather (Boris) writes to a business colleague (Karl) about his visit to his daughter's family. You may need to research German names and customs. Include references to:

- the money he has to pay to support them;
- how the apartment looked;
- thoughts about his daughter;
- how Hans (the son) looked and thoughts about the railroad;
- the Jewish family upstairs and his prejudice;
- thoughts about his son-in-law (Sebastian).

The tone of the letter should be: pompous, self-satisfied, arrogant, mean and small-minded.

In the re-drafting process it may be necessary to do some work on how you can make a letter sound like the character – many pupils pick this up quite quickly and easily.

Frau Schneider (Ingrid) writes to her sister (Heidi): Include references to:

- Friedrich and his first day at school;
- the paper bag;
- the amusement park – the merry-go-round, cotton candy, licorice, swing boats, the photo, the horse and the laughter;
- the Richters and Hans.

The tone of the letter should be: happy, have a sense of well-being. cheerful, loving, modest, prosperous and generous.

13 HOMEWORK – etymological research.

Discover the origin of boycott.

14 Create two spider plans around the concepts of PROSPERITY and POVERTY.

Design a graph which traces the two families and their fortunes in terms of PROSPERITY and POVERTY.

15 HOMEWORK – think about all the different types of religion there are in the world.

16 In small groups prepare a reading of one of these chapters:

The Jungvolk, The Ball, Conversation on the Stairs and Herr Schneider.

After reading

17 Write a pamphlet about PREJUDICE, include:

- general information,
- different types of prejudice,
- ideas about reducing or stopping prejudice.

18 Divide the class into the staffs of two newspapers, one jewish and the other Nazi. Write reports about the following events:

- the picket outside the shop (pp 29–31);
- the breaking of the shop window (pp 38–41);

19 Write a letter from Friedrich to Helga explaining why he cannot see her anymore.

Assessment

Examinations are formidable
(Charles Colton, Lacon)

- Explain work and mark schemes to your pupils.
- Ask pupils for ideas to improve assessment criteria.
- Ask pupils to work out marking schemes for self and peer assessment.
- Make assessment both pupil and teacher friendly with short answer or completion questions.
- Keep clear records which give you an immediate picture of pupil performance.
- Ensure that there is room on worksheets for written feedback to pupils, or use a feedback slip.
- Be sensitive when you return assessed work. Make your first comments a joy to receive.
- Do you need grades, marks or scores? Alphabetic or numerical grades can dominate pupils' reactions and encourage unproductive comparisons.
- Use an informative symbolic mark scheme and supportive comments rather than crosses and ticks (see *Malet Lambert School English Faculty Mark Scheme*, page 50).
- Give pupils an opportunity to discard their weaker efforts and build on formative assessment – six out of eight assignments for an overall grade.

Marking scheme

Malet Lambert School
English Faculty
Marking Scheme

Your English teacher will use the symbols below to show you where there are mistakes in your written work. Please correct any mistakes when you redraft your writing.

Marginal	Instruction	Textual Mark
SP	Check spelling of underlined word	<u>Lundun</u>
P	Check punctuation	(⋅)
MP	Insert missing punctuation	∧
SL	Change to small letter	<u>T</u>ree
CL	Change to capital letter	<u>k</u>atherine
BP	Begin a new paragraph	//
⸙	Run two paragraphs together	⸙
NW	Insert an appropriate word	∧
CT	Change to correct tense	<u>play</u>
E	Check use of English	We <u>was</u> playing
WW	Wrong word	~~played~~

ECM

Self and peer assessment

Animals are such agreeable friends – they ask no questions, they pass no criticisms
(George Eliot, Mr Gilfril's Love Story)

- Self and peer assessment help pupils to be aware of the way the formal assessment system works.
- Self-assessment encourages pupils to look closely at what they are asked to do.
- Encourage pupils to own assessment. Help them to draw up an assessment schedule for a piece or a sequence of work.
- No scores – only comments.
- Never remark self-assessment. Moderate the quality of the assessment.
- Peer assessment has the double benefit of a pupil's own response plus a further analysis of the task during the assessment process.
- Choose tasks where the process of feeding back is a part of the assessor's learning process.
- Work as a 'consultant' to moderate the assessment process.
- Act as a conciliation and arbitration service when there are problems.

Pupil self-assessment sheet*

Science

Pupil Name: _____

Tutor Group: _____

Teacher: _____ Date: _____

Grades:
Achievement _____
Effort _____

How much effort are they putting into: (1 = excellent 4 = poor)	1		2		3		4	
	Teacher	Pupil	Teacher	Pupil	Teacher	Pupil	Teacher	Pupil
Learning key ideas								
Planning experiments								
Observing and measuring accurately								
Writing conclusions								
Written work								
Class discussion work								
Completing and handing in homework								

Target for improvement

Signatures _____

*Based on a pupil self-assessment sheet in use at Oaklands School, York.

Designing active learning materials

Let a single complete action, in one place and one day, keep the theatre packed to the last
(Nicholas Boileau, L'Art Poetique)

- Active learning materials encourage pupils to work through the curriculum at their own pace.

- Identify those areas of the curriculum where pupils can manage their own learning and give clear learning objectives.

- Ensure that your materials contain sufficient tasks to stimulate pupils.

- Ensure that your instructions are clear.

- Ensure that pupils can assess their own work and receive feedback before they move on.

- Ask some of your pupils and pupils from other classes to try out your materials – market research is essential for a pupil-friendly product.

- As well as self/peer assessment include a control test which you mark. This will help you to monitor the progress of pupils and materials.

- Explain to pupils the place and purpose of active learning materials in your scheme of work.

- Keep hard copy as well as computer discs and rewrite as often as necessary.

Writing worksheets and handouts

True ease in writing comes from art, not chance
(Alexander Pope, An Essay on Criticism)

- Make an immediate impact with pictures and illustrations which support your message (see *The Volunteer*, page 55).

- Use a customised template to create an interesting house style (see *40 Love*, page 56).

- Always word process your handouts using simple fonts such as Courier, Helvetica or Lucida Bright.

- Create interactive worksheets by asking pupils to do things which engage their interest (see *How Have I Been Since You Last Saw Me?* page 57).

- Include blank spaces for pupil responses (see *Decorated for a Kiss*, page 58).

- Ensure that each worksheet is self contained, or clearly a part of a well ordered sequence.

- Write clear headings and instruction.

- Write worksheets which help pupils to work at home.

- Include a formative assessment so that pupils understand what they have achieved and what else they need to do to reach their learning objectives.

- Store your worksheets on disc so that you can update, or tailor them to meet specific needs.

The Volunteer worksheet

The Read through *The Volunteer* two or three times. Then underline those words, in the first verse, which describe the clerk's life (a) as it was, (b) as he dreamt it could be.

The Volunteer

Here lies a clerk who half his life had spent
Toiling at ledgers in a city grey,
Thinking that so his days would drift away
With no lance broken in life's tournament.
Yet over twixt the books and his bright eyes
The gleaming eagles of the legions came,
And horsemen, charging under phantom skies,
Went thundering past beneath the oriflamme.

And now those waiting dreams are satisfied;
From twilight to the halls of dawn he went;
His lance is broken; but he lies content
With that high hour; in which he lived and died.
And falling thus he wants no recompense,
Who found his battle in the last resort;
Nor need he any hearse to bear him hence,
Who goes to join the men of Agincourt.

Herbert Asquith

In a small group talk about the groups of words (a) and (b).
How do they differ?

1 In your own words, explain briefly why the clerk volunteered.

2 Look again at those words which you underlined. Why might the poet have chosen to use those particular words?

3 Look closely at the way the poet uses individual words and phrases in the second verse. How does he manage to show his readers that the volunteer died happily?

40-Love worksheet

Often, the best way to understand a poem is to read it aloud. How exactly should it be read?

Why has the poet decided to put it like that? What does he want to put across to the reader?

In pairs, decide how best to read this poem aloud to the rest of your class.

40 – Love

middle	aged
couple	playing
ten-	nis
when	the
game	ends
and	they
go	home
the	net
will	still
be	be-
tween	them

Roger McGough

After reading

1 How is the arrangement of the words on the page linked with the subject of the poem?

2 What does the gap in the middle of the poem represent?

Suggestion for writing

Write a story in which the net is still between the players after the game. How might they behave towards each other? What will they knock backwards and forwards now?

Where have I been since you last saw me? worksheet

In order to grasp the sense or meaning of this poem you are going to be asked to remove most of the words – leaving only key words or phrases

The words you choose to leave should provide a skeletal message, around which the rest of the poem fits. For example, in the first four lines you might decide to leave only the words in *italics*.

How Have I Been Since You Last Saw Me?

Well,
      I've never been *lonely*
      I've danced at *parties*,
      and drunk *flat* beer
with other men;
      I've been to the cinema and seen
      one or two films you would have liked
with other men;
      I've passed the time in amusement arcades
      and had one or two pretty fruitless
      goes on fruit machines;
      I've memorised the patterns
      of miscellaneous neckties.
Indifferent, I
      put varying amounts of sugar
in different coffee cups
      and adjusted myself to divers heights
      of assorted goodnight kisses, but
my breasts (once bitten)
      shy away from contact
I keep a curb
      on mind and body -
Love?   I'm no longer
      exposing myself.

Liz Lochhead

Suggestion for writing   Write a dialogue between two friends who have met for the first time since one of them left/was dumped by a boy/girl friend.

Decorated for a Kiss worksheet

The last part of each line in this poem has been removed. In a group, build up the poem by choosing an ending for each line from the box below. Write your chosen ending in the space provided.

Decorated for a Kiss

I come to her house for love...

Men-friend tell me...

Come, man, come fish shark, ...

At midnight come...

But I decide my mind ....

Her dress is...

She has put...

Green lizards run..

Her body has the scent...

The sweet fibres she ....

She has washed ....

She has rubbed..

She has made..

Now...

---

her lips with bay leaves, what a fool to go to the girl, in her eyes, with a basket of red petals, of sun-dried khus khus grass, fish golden snapper along the warm black rocks, and come to her for love, a red bead in each ear, her limbs clean with water from a green calabash, patterned with blue dragon-flies, her mouth with milk, she has put between the linen since midday

---

The whole of the last line of the poem is missing. When you have completed the rest of the poem, write your own last line.

When you have finished ask for a copy of the original poem.

Writing reports

Report me and my cause aright
(William Shakespeare, Hamlet)

- Prepare for report writing by keeping accurate, informative records.

- Build up an assessment portfolio for each pupil. This will inform your report writing and provide evidence to show parents.

- Write a first draft, leave it for a while before completing the final version.

- If photographs are available, have them close at hand as you write.

- Use photographs to ensure that you are writing about the correct pupil.

- Use a pupil's preferred name on her report.

- Say something positive first – this makes the bitter pill easier to swallow.

- Write legibly or word process your reports. Use the spell checker.

- Avoid clichés and sterile statement banks. Write about your pupils.

- Ensure that each pupil knows what is in her report before it goes home.

Chapter 3

Rules and relationships

The golden rule is that there are no golden rules
(G.B. Shaw, Man and Superman)

Animal and human relationships are governed by rules. Some, such as the Rules of Golf, are explicit. They are available to all players in a written form. Any player who breaks these rules is penalised. Other sets of rules, or codes of conduct, are implicit, unspoken, uncodified. Hens, for example, have a pecking order.

Rules in schools can be of both kinds – making the management of relationships complicated. There are explicit, implicit, national, local, school and classroom rules. The National Curriculum is set out in an Act of Parliament. Regulations for educational visits are laid down by Local Education Authorities. Dress codes can be agreed by school governing bodies. Then there are the teacher's rules for the classroom, designed to control movement, personal space and work.

The rules of societies and the relationships of their members are interconnected and indivisible. In both formal and informal contexts the relationship between two or more people will be affected by the rules of the game. Football players may not kick each other. Families regulate their use of the bathroom, mealtimes and other shared activities according to rules generated through long term, informal negotiation.

When relationships break down, it is often because the rules of the game are seen to be unfair or inconsistently applied, or because there has been insufficient negotiation resulting in dissent. The effective classroom manager can minimise dissent by helping pupils to understand their important contribution to all classroom processes. They must also understand that two yellow cards lead to an early bath (see *Roscow Fold Key Stage 1 Classroom Plan,* page 67).

Extreme, inappropriate behaviour can lead to a loss of control – every teacher's worst nightmare. If you cannot establish a suitable physical and social environment within your classroom you will not be able to teach. Your pupils will not be able to learn.

Fortunately, most inappropriate behaviour is trivial. Pupils talk too much. They don't pay sufficient attention. They don't concentrate. They wander round the classroom. They interfere with other pupils' possessions.

These trivial behaviours can be eliminated or controlled by prevention. The bedrock of prevention is preparation. 'Fail to prepare and you prepare to fail' is always true in the classroom. The effective classroom manager prepares pupils to behave appropriately by clarifying all school and classroom rules. They establish, cooperatively, with their pupils the rights and responsibilities of everyone connected with that classroom and the school. They define the procedures and routines that make their classroom work. This can eliminate most of the inappropriate behaviours that arise when pupils don't know the rules of the game.

Preventing disruption

Discipline must be maintained
(Charles Dickens, Bleak House*)*

The effective classroom manager will always try to prevent disruption rather than contain it.

- Invite pupils to draw up a class code of conduct (see *Kelvin Hall High School Classroom Charter,* page 64)
- Provide instant rewards for good behaviour.
- Avoid confrontations. A quiet word works wonders.
- Link breaches of the class code of conduct with known, reasonable sanctions.
- Plan to avoid disruptions by providing suitable work for all of your pupils (see *Differentiation,* page 41).
- Involve pupils in target setting.
- Change to Plan 'B', 'C' or 'D' if your original lesson plan is not working.
- Isolate problem pupils.
- Build 'time out' into the class code of conduct (see *Roscow Fold Key Stage 1 Classroom Plan,* page 67).
- Spend some quality time with the problem pupils to find out the reason for their inappropriate behaviour.
- Always have something interesting at hand to fill a cooling off period – an emergency quiz can work.

Positive discipline

I have submitted to a new control
(William Wordsworth, Elegiac Stanzas)

- Provide pupils with copies of school and classroom rules, responsibilities and rights (see *Kelvin Hall High School Parent, Pupil and Teacher Responsibilities*, page 65).

- Adapt and use standard health and safety signs to provide pupils with visual guidance.

- Discuss with pupils the reasonable and logical consequences of any inappropriate behaviour. Emphasise that these consequences will follow a decision to behave inappropriately.

- Before you react to inappropriate behaviour – pause, reflect, ask yourself is it a first offense?

- Always monitor the mood of your class, be flexible, allow some fidget time.

- Consistency create a comfort zone – ensure that pupils understand what you expect.

- Try to be aware of any extenuating circumstances.

    Is the pupil seeking attention?

    Does the pupil suffer from an attention deficit?

    Is unchallenging work causing a problem?

    Is the pupil frustrated through lack of understanding?

    Has the pupil finished his work?

    Does the pupil know what to do next?

    Is the pupil having trouble concentrating?

    Is the pupil mounting a challenge to your authority?

- Any remedy will probably involve some change in classroom organisation.

Classroom Charter

Classroom Charter

ALL MEMBERS OF THE CLASS HAVE A RIGHT TO:

1 be themselves
2 equal opportunities
3 speak and be heard without interruption
4 work without interference
5 a healthy and safe working environment
6 their own privacy and property
7 respect
8 ask questions
9 stimulating lessons
10 make mistakes without being ridiculed
11 support to enable them to learn to the best of their ability
12 be free from racial, religious, sexual and social harassment.

Parent, pupil and teacher responsibilities

The following sets of responsibilities were produced as part of a Year 7 Induction Evening.

Parents should

- be consistent, fair and honest
- ensure that pupils adhere to the school dress code
- ensure that pupils have a quiet area for homework and
- ensure that pupils attend school
- ensure that pupils are well fed and rested
- praise, support and encourage
- share quality time
- be available to discuss problems
- have a sense of humour

Pupils should

- be consistent, fair and honest
- work hard
- respect others and their property
- obey school rules
- listen to others and not interrupt

Teacher should

- be consistent, fair and honest
- be well organised
- prepare and teach differentiated lessons
- apply the school rules
- have a sense of humour
- realistic about work loads
- not punish a whole class for one pupil's misbehaviour
- no punish pupils in public

Reprimands

*Having been a little chastised, they shall be greatly rewarded
(Old Testament, Wisdom of Solomon)*

- Pupils perform positively when praised.

- Let your pupils know the rules of your classroom when you first meet them (see *Roscow Fold Primary School Key Stage 1 Classroom Plan*, page 67). Discuss rules, draw up a class code of conduct. Remember ownership can help pupils understand and meet behavioural targets.

- Whenever possible reprimand pupils immediately.

- Don't waste words

    Tell pupils exactly what they have done wrong.

    Refer to the class code of conduct.

- Tell pupils exactly how you feel about their inappropriate behaviour.

- Don't rush on.

    Let pupils feel uncomfortable, for a moment or two, about what they have done wrong. Ask them how they feel about their behaviour.

- End on a positive note. Let pupils know that you value them and their positive contributions.

- When the reprimand is finished say so.

The Classroom Plan

Here are the rules for Key Stage 1 at Roscow Fold V.C. Primary School in Bolton.

The Classroom Plan

Rules
1 Follow directions.
2 Be kind to each other.
3 Take care of everything.
4 Ask permission before leaving the room.

Rewards for appropriate behaviour

1 Praise.
2 Stickers and badges.
3 Certificates to take home.
4 Friday book.
5 Merit cup.
6 Sent to Headteacher (for reinforcement of praise).
7 Class and group rewards.

Consequences following inappropriate behaviour

1 A warning.
2 'Time out' in class.
3 Last out for playtime.
4 Speak to parent.
5 Sent to Headteacher.

Reinforcement

In nature there are neither rewards or punishments - there are consequences.
(R.G. Ingersoll, Lectures and Essays)

- Pupils perform positively when praised.
- Let your pupils know when you first meet them that you are going to tell how they are progressing.
- Praise your pupils often.
- Tell your pupils what they have done right.
- Tell your pupils that you value their contributions, especially when they have helped the whole class to progress.
- Don't rush on. Let pupils bask in the warm glow of approbation.
- Encourage pupils to build upon what they have done and make further positive contributions to lessons.
- Encourage pupils to praise each other.
- Introduce the concept of the 'critical friend'. A respected person who has the ability to provide support through encouragement and is able to deliver difficult messages when necessary.

School Letters

---

*School
_____

Address

Date

Dear Parent/Guardian

Today your son, Jason's behaviour in class was so poor that he was sent out of a lesson (s).

As a result, he will be placed on report for 10 school days.

Each night the report will be presented to me a 3.15 pm for signature.

If the report is unsatisfactory in any way, there will be an immediate ten minute detention.

Persistent failure to behave whilst on report will result in a formal one hour detention of which you will be notified in writing.

Please complete the form below and return it to the school to show that you have received this letter.

Yours sincerely

Form Tutor/Head of Year

- -

Pupil Name   *Form*

I have received your letter regarding the report. I support the school in its actions. _____

Name _____   *Signature* _____

Date _____

---

*Based on a letter in use at William Gee School, Hull.

School

Address

Date

Dear Parent/Guardian

As you know, form tutors deal with daily disciplinary problems within school.

However, Sarah's form tutor is so concerned about her current situation that s/he has referred the matter to me.

I would be grateful if you could contact me to discuss the situation.

I am usually available to take telephone calls between 8.00 – 8.30 am, 12.30 am – 1.00 pm and from 3.45 until 4.30 pm each day.

Yours sincerely

Head of Year

School

Address

Date

Dear Parent/Guardian

I am writing to congratulate your son, William, on achieving 98% attendance in the first half of this year. If this continues he will achieve his compact goal of 90% attendance in a year. It is very important that pupils attend regularly and we are pleased to note your son's good record so far. We hope that he keeps it up.

Well done!

Yours sincerely

Head of Year

Duties

Do the duty that lies nearest thee, which thou knowest to be a duty!
(Thomas Carlyle, Sartor Resartus)

The classroom is where it happens, but break and lunch times create more flash points than lessons.

- Save your voice. Get a whistle. A whistle can cut through most noise and command attention.

- Know the rules. Read school policies. Find an experienced colleague to shadow you before you go it alone.

- Adopt a high profile. There's no point patrolling unless you make an impact in no-man's-land!

- Be vigilant and prevent trouble.

- Enter danger zones, such as smokers' corner, loudly – this allows the usual suspects to adopt positive attitudes. Remember, prevention is better than punishment.

- Wear something warm, arrange for delivery of a hot drink. Ensure that your after-break lesson is well set up.

- Know the school's emergency routines: who does First Aid and how to contact them?

- Only use reasonable force to break up fights.

- Talk to pupils – build up good relationships.

Chapter 4

Supporting pupils with learning difficulties

Tis not enough to help the feeble up, But to support him after
(William Shakespeare, Timon of Athens)

In order to help pupils with learning difficulties, effective classroom managers need to look at changes in teaching and learning strategies, not at changing pupils. They need to determine where a pupil's learning difficulty is, and identify the cause.

This diagnosis can be made by a primary class teacher or a secondary subject specialist. As effective classroom managers they will have developed both the generic and the specialist skills to support pupils. These packages, with a variety of differentiated outcomes, can ensure that all pupils are able to attempt related tasks and enjoy some success.

Good support, like good teaching, begins with high teacher expectation. This is the single most effective way teachers can support their pupils.

Any teacher who sees pupils as failures, lacking significant skills, or is satisfied with a downward spiral of testing and labelling, will demotivate them. The effective classroom manager will motivate and increase self-esteem through differentiated tasks analysed to ensure that each stage, and each strategy, is clearly defined in terms that are easily understood.

This shift of expectation from failure to success, coupled with positive learning experiences, can lead pupils to believe in themselves. It can convince them that they can learn.

ECM

Collaborative learning

The gods help them that help themselves
(Aesop, Hercules and the Waggoner)

Pupils can help each other to make enormous leaps in understanding when they explain, in their language, a piece of knowledge or a process. Working together can also enhance problem solving skills and promote an inclusive classroom culture.

- Explain to pupils the reasons for working together and the expected benefits of cooperation.
- Plan activities which reduce competition and promote cooperation.
- Show pupils how to share expertise as well as tasks.
- Teach pupils to ask and answer questions, especially the big question which can resolve a problem, so that they do not feel threatened.
- Create opportunities for pupils to teach each other.
- Use random, mixed, ability-based and friendship groups to balance or unbalance the spread of skills and abilities for specific learning targets.
- Don't create problems by insisting that pupils who never get on with each other work together. Chip away at the problem.
- Have a contingency plan in case of problems.
- Monitor group performance to avoid lurkers.
- Plan time for groups to share their experience.

Supporting pupils - Maths

*Mathematics possesses not only truth, but supreme beauty
(Bertrand, Lord Russell, The Study of Mathematics)*

Unimaginative teaching can make maths the most difficult
subject to learn. An effective classroom manager can make
maths more accessible to all pupils by avoiding drudgery. It is
important to make maths fun whenever possible.

- Make maths real – use everyday examples such as APR,
  cricket scoring, league tables, shopping and wages.

- Maths is like the Tour de France – you have to successfully
  complete stage one before you can start stage two. If you
  miss a stage you'll never see Paris.

- Train pupils to do detective work – they can identify
  errors and suggest solutions.

- Slowly, slowly gets the right answer – accuracy not speed
  is vital.

- Encourage pupils to share success and explain how they
  got it right.

- Use peer assessment as a learning experience.

- Adopt a problem solving approach through group work
  whenever possible.

- Provide lots of differentiated material.

- Get the basics right before moving onto *exciting*, further
  maths.

- Practise makes perfect – just do it often!

Supporting pupils – Reading

Reading is to the mind what exercise is to the body
(Sir Richard Steele, The Tatler)

In a culture where assessment and communication are based on the written, rather than spoken, word reading difficulties can be a severe educational, personal and social handicap. The effective classroom manager can help alleviate these problems by following this simple scheme.

- Support pupils who have reading difficulties and create opportunities to increase their self-esteem.
- Give oral as well as written instructions.
- Promote a supportive atmosphere in which pupils can ask for instructions to be repeated.
- Identify pupils who have reading problems. Liaise with the SENCO to arrange diagnostic testing and support.
- 'Be short, be simple, be human' (Sir Ernest Gowers). Plain English makes information accessible to everyone.
- Avoid a mismatch between pupils' listening and reading abilities and your own style of speaking and writing.
- Keep it simple – use one main idea per sentence when speaking and writing.
- Teach new vocabulary to improve learning and assessment opportunities.
- Use a variety of forms of assessment to avoid discrimination.
- Use the Hawthorne Effect to increase motivation (the tendency for any change introduced into a work environment to bring about a temporary increase in productivity simply because change has been made).

Revision

*If you are truly serious about preparing your child for the future,
don't teach him to subtract – teach him to deduct
(Fran Lebowitz, Social Studies)*

Few people will have any direct experience of preparing for
examinations. When helping them to get ready for public or school
exams it is important to stress that there are no hard and fast
rules. As with all study skills, pupils need to try things out and see
what suits them, what fits in with their way of working and their
lifestyle.

- Ensure that pupils understand that throwing time at
  revision is not a good idea – quality time is best.
- Teach pupils to prepare revision aids as their course
  progresses.
- Introduce pupils to exam questions, teach them to break
  questions into manageable chunks.
- Make revision fun with programmes such as *A Question of
  Economic History*.
- Deconstruct past papers to show pupils how questions
  work and ways in which marks can be won.
- Provide mark schemes so that pupils can assess each
  others' work.
- Teach pupils how to actively revise rather than read
  passively – application of knowledge is essential.
- Introduce pupils to a variety of learning styles so that they
  can pick and mix to suit themselves.
- Show pupils how to create 10 point summaries of any
  topic they need to know.
- Supervise the preparation of timed revision plans which
  include fun and relaxation.
- Teach pupils to visualise a confident, successful
  examination performance.

Passing examinations

Do not on any account attempt to write on both sides of the paper at once
(W.C. Sellar and R.J. Yeatman, 1066 and All That)

Pupils' confidence can be increased and tension reduced through systematic revision and structured examination practice. The following strategies will help pupils to understand that success is a product of knowledge, revision and application.

- Set a positive tone with the mantra – preparation plus practise produces a pass.
- Build confidence by introducing pupils to parts and whole questions from the start of their course.
- Practise with class and homework sessions.
- Relate examination success to real life experiences such as the Driving Test.
- Practise makes proficient – write exam answers.
- Introduce pupils to time management as a lifeskill.
- Conduct exam surgeries in which groups work out what the examiner is asking for.
- Train pupils to identify the leading language of a question: compare and contrast, describe, discuss.
- Train pupils to read the exam paper carefully and make sensible decisions about the questions they answer.
- Make a plan on the exam paper before writing an answer.
- Move on to another question if stuck.
- Examiners respond well to clear, well presented work.
- Include editing time in the exam plan.

Creativity

I will not Reason and Compare; my business is to Create
(William Blake, Jerusalem)

Both the National Curriculum and examination syllabuses can lead to tunnel vision. targets and questions, questions and targets. You can widen your pupils' perspective and enhance their peripheral vision.

- Don't be blinkered by targets.

- Encourage pupils to approach problems from different directions.

- Avoid closed questions with yes/no or *right* answers. Ask open-ended questions which leave room for *different* answers. Celebrate unexpected outcomes.

- Answers to difficult questions aren't always comfortable. Encourage pupils to consider extreme solutions.

- Look for positive points in all responses.

- Encourage pupils to approach problems in their own way. Let them learn from experience before you show them the *right* way.

- Few people or groups solve complex problems without spending time on dead end ideas or unworkable solutions. Use rough work and drafting to show pupils that process is as important as product.

- Show people how to collect and sift ideas through spider plans and brainstorming.

Writing Essays

This of course is not what he was trying to say, but the pen is mightier than the wrist.
(A.E.Housman, Classical Review)

The purpose of an essay, whether it is a coursework assignment or an examination answer, is to explain a topic by presenting ideas and reasons supported by various forms of evidence.

Good writing has a beginning, middle and end. A good essay has an introduction, development and conclusion. The introduction tells the reader what will follow in the development – which argues the case – before the conclusion sums it up.

The effective classroom manager can help pupils to write better essays with this routine.

- Show pupils how to turn a question into a statement framing a strong answer.
- Train pupils to use a spider plan to explore ideas and produce a list of points to be turned into the paragraphs of their essay.
- Teach pupils to eliminate the irrelevant and logically sequence relevant ideas to produce an essay plan.
- Make pupils aware of the key words, such as *compare* and *contrast*, which appear in examination questions and essay titles.

    Compare – look for similarities.

    Contrast – examine differences.

- Train pupils to sum up what they have. Whenever possible they should write a strong conclusion.
- Train pupils to revise their introductions to fit what they have written.
- Encourage pupils to redraft their writing to create a vigorous style.
- Provide opportunities for pupils to read their essays to a small group of critical friends.

Homework

Weary with the labour of our journeys, we return home and rest on the couch
(Catallus, Carmina iii)

Well designed homework tasks, linked to classwork, allow pupils to develop independence and the capacity to work on their own. Parents can see what their children are doing at school and support their learning.

- Make homework a positive activity by encouraging pupils and parents to follow **The homework plan** on page 83.
- Carefully prepared homework, clearly explained and promptly returned to pupils, is most useful.
- Use homework to consolidate prior learning or research a fresh topic.
- Always follow the school homework policy.
- As a part of your closing routine, remind pupils about homework.
- Collect homework at the set time – this encourages pupils to value it.
- Do not set homework tasks which require access to dictionaries or other books which may not be available at home.
- Encourage parents and pupils to set a space aside for quiet work away from distractions such as television and siblings.
- If resources are available organise a homework club so that all pupils have access to a quiet space, reference books, computers and advice.
- Train pupils to keep a simple homework record in their exercise books.
- Dogs rarely eat homework – no excuses.

The homework plan

Prepared for the accelerated learning group at North Ferriby CE Primary School.

1 Do your homework at the same time very night.

2 Until you acquire discipline, work where your parents can supervise you.

3 Make a work plan before you start.

4 Take a break every half an hour.

5 Turn off the television.

6 Do the most difficult work first.

7 Work in an uncluttered area.

8 If you use a computer, spell check your work.

9 Proof read or sense check all of your work.

10 Reward yourself with a treat when your homework is done.

Giving clear directions

How does it feel/To be on your own/With no direction...
(Bob Dylan, Like a Rolling Stone)

Explaining, instructing and giving directions is a large part of what teachers do. No matter how you give directions, some pupils won't get the message.

- Always follow your established routine for giving directions.
- Deliver directions from a given place in the classroom. Some teachers stand on a coloured carpet tile as a signal that something important is about to be said, others stand under a star or halo suspended from the ceiling.
- Wait until all of your pupils are listening to you.
- Tell the class what you are going to give them directions about. Give your directions. Test understanding by asking pupils to repeat parts of your message.
- Avoid imprecise language, quantities and timings. Say, you have five minutes to complete this rather than spend a few moments...
- Don't ask: 'Does everyone understand?'
- Ask pupils to explain your instructions to a response partner.
- Invite questions about your instructions.
- If your directions concern a task to be completed over a series of lessons or in a given time, list the directions as bullet points on a time chart so that pupils have something to refer to as they work.
- Don't make a habit of repeating the directions to individuals. This discourages active listening.
- If a significant number of pupils seem confused by your directions review your message. Does it need to be delivered in a different way?

Working partners and groups

Committee: a group of men who individually can do nothing but as a group decide that nothing can be done
(Fred Allen, Quotations for Our Time)

Classroom or playground pick-up groups and teams always leave someone isolated as last choice. This can be a severe blow to a pupil's self esteem and stressful for the pupils making the selection. It is important to use a variety of mechanisms for creating partnerships or groups.

- Allocate medium to long term response partners who can read through drafts and answer questions.
- Pick names or register numbers out of a bag.
- Hand out playing cards and match the numbers as partners or in groups of four.
- Match opposite ends of the alphabet. A works with Z, B with Y.
- Create random pairings or groups by asking pupils to pick numbered cards – the 1s work together.
- Sometimes you will want to create ability, problem solving or skill centred groups. Do this in advance and tell the class that they will be working in groups. Put up a list of groups. If necessary indicate a chair and note taker.
- If pupils have a genuine reason for not working with a particular person, or group, listen carefully and talk the issue through before making a decision.
- Allocate new pupils to partners or groups who will be supportive.

Effective tutoring

I am putting old heads on your young shoulders... all my pupils are the creme de la creme
(Muriel Spark, The Prime of Miss Jean Brodie)

- Pupils are individuals, not members of a class. Learn their names, characteristics and idiosyncrasies.

- Know your pupils and their *normal* personas – recognise abnormal behaviour in order to resolve problems before they happen.

- Make form time quality time. Be available and talk to form members about things that matter – home, school and street life.

- Be inclusive – encourage a form feeling through group activities which require pupils to work together. Don't always allow them to work in social groups. Explain the necessity of skill and specialist support groups.

- Know individuals and avoid sensitive issues. You can collect information by teaching pupils how to complete questionnaires.

- Create a form base and good team spirit, build a 'we are the champions' feeling, without being aggressively competitive or elitist.

- Be your form's facilitator/conciliator – intercede when they get into trouble and make school life easier, smoother, happier.

- Celebrate together – keep an anniversary and birthday book.

- Help pupils to acquire positive social skills.

- Keep administration to a minimum. Don't allow intrusions into form time.

Form tutors' checklist

Form tutors have numerous responsibilities, including:

Administration	Skills	Training
1 Registration	Effective Management	In-house INSET
2 Dinner numbers	Effective communication	Mentoring
3 Attendance records and returns		
4 Checking homework diaries		
5 Communicating with parents		
6 Collecting/collating reply slips from parents		

Group Work		
7 Form time	Interactive skills	Role play
8 Personal & Social Education including		INSET
9 ■ Bully watch		Shadowing an experienced tutor
10 ■ Equal opportunities implementation		
11 ■ Alcohol & drug abuse programmes		
12 ■ Sex education		

Interpersonal		
13 Problem Solving	Listening	An introduction to basic counselling by a trained provider
	Decision making	

Quality Assurance		
14 Collecting data from subject teachers	Counselling	INSET
15 Delivering feedback to pupils	Basic educational	ITT & INSET
16 Target setting	psychology	
17 Providing reports for parents		
18 Delivering feedback to parents		
■ by telephone		
■ by letter		
■ at consultation evenings		

Encouraging pupils to talk

*I do not object to people looking at their watches when I am
speaking. But I strongly object when they start shaking them to make
certain they are still going.*
(Lord Birkett, in the Observer)

- It's good to talk but it's even better when you listen.
  Talking one-to-one means that both you and your pupil
  can concentrate.
- Try teacher's question time in which pupils ask
  parliamentary style questions with supplementary
  questions to get the answer they want.
- Set up a brains trust in which pupils answer each other's
  questions.
- Soften the blow when pupils give incorrect answers. Let
  them know that an answer has room for development –
  brainstorm a solution.
- Use you dramatic skills to convince pupils that you do not
  know the answer.
- Adopt a Jeremy Paxman persona to pursue a point and pin
  pupils down.
- Be a professional researcher for your pupils – they ask,
  you find out.
- Ask pupils to draw up a list of 'things we need to know'.
  Individuals, pairs and small groups can provide answers.
- Provide opportunities for pupils to ask you questions in a
  variety of roles: informed adult, socially aware observer,
  expert and so on.
- Treat everything seriously – there's no such thing as an
  irrelevant question or comment. Turn a negative into a
  positive learning experience.
- Draw in outsiders and quiet members of the class by
  giving them specific roles as presenters, questioners or
  researchers.
- Hot seat members of your class to talk about themselves
  and their interests.

Enhancing self-esteem

I am a doormat in a world of boots
(Jean Rhys, in The Guardian*)*

- Confidence and self-esteem develop through success. Provide all pupils with opportunities to be successful.

- Encourage pupils to congratulate each other and celebrate success.

- Give negative feedback privately and avoid pejorative terms (see 'Whatsoever things are true', page 26).

- Help pupils to build on their strengths by keeping a record of successes. Ask them what they know, not what they don't know.

- Show pupils that weaknesses are undeveloped strengths. Plan to reduce or eradicate the weaknesses.

- Show pupils that problems are merely waiting for solutions. Weaknesses are opportunities for growth which will produce self-esteem.

- Talk about lack of achievement in a non-threatening way. Show pupils that nobody emerges as a finished product. People acquire skills and develop talents as they grow – give illustrations such as Einstein.

- Encourage pupils to grade days and achievements like the heroine in Judy Blume's *It's Not the End of the World*. They can share A+ and C– moments.

- Ask pupils to share things which make them feel good about themselves. They may find positive points of which they were previously unaware.

- Create a file of differentiated feelgood activities which will allow pupils to succeed and be seen as successful by their peers.

Helping pupils to handle emotions

Undisciplined squads of emotions
(T.S. Eliot, Burnt Norton*)*

- Your experience of 'undisciplined squads of emotions' can help pupils.
- New pressures can prevent learning. Help pupils to reduce pressure.
- Get to the root of the problem through gentle probing.
- Counsel, don't interrogate. Create openings for pupils to explain.
- Softly ask the big question. Why are you angry? What's made you cry? Listen and support. Don't be judgmental.
- Listen, support, but don't accept symptoms as causes.
- In a safe environment, encourage pupils to express their emotions.
- Through Personal and Social Education encourage pupils to see strong feelings as normal. Emphasise that subsequent experiences can be easier as each individual learns to cope.
- Explain your coping strategies. Talk about times when you have needed to express strong feelings.
- Role play can help pupils to make emotions into positive experiences by:
     regarding emotions as strong signals;
     collecting a set of coping strategies.
- Develop support systems amongst your colleagues. Draw on the available pool of talent . Who is a good listener, a natural counsellor?
- Don't be afraid to call in the experts. Do be diplomatic and avoid stigmatising pupils.

Breaking bad news

Though it be honest, it is never good
To bring bad news
(William Shakespeare, Antony and Cleopatra*)*

- Bad news has to be broken by someone – one day it may be you. Do you need a bereavement counselling course? (Contact Cruse, Cruse House, 126 Sheen Road, Richmond, Surrey, TW9 1UR.)
- Don't break bad news until you are sure of the facts. If you receive news by telephone, call the pupil's contact number to check details.
- Prepare a short script so that you get it right. Have relevant contact telephone numbers available.
- Never act alone. Ask a colleague of the opposite sex to yourself to assist.
- Prepare an informal, private location in which to break the news.
- Be prepared for the aftermath. What has to be done once you have broken the news? Will the pupil need to be taken home? Will a relative or known adult collect the pupil?
- Use a subterfuge to get the pupil concerned out of the classroom and into a private place... 'please take this note to Mr A in Room 1'.
- Be gentle, do not prevaricate. Ask the pupil to sit down. Use your script to keep to the point... 'I'm sorry, Name, I've got some bad news for you'.
- Be ready for an emotional response. Help your pupil to cry if necessary. Comfort such as hand holding or hugging can be given by a colleague of the same sex as the pupil.
- Ask the pupil whether you should let the class know about the news. Do not give details. Do not break a confidence.
- Let your colleagues know that the pupil concerned needs to be treated sensitively – there is no need to be specific.
- Keep in touch with the pupil and their family in case they need support.

Bereavement counselling

All Life death does end and each day dies with sleep
(Gerald Manley Hopkins, No Worst, there is none)

Pupils need support as they mourn and come to terms with their loss. After a death, there are mourning tasks to accomplish to restore an equilibrium.

1 Do show respect by active listening:

- be courteous and adopt an attentive posture
- make eye contact, reflecting facial expression
- nod your head in agreement
- use your pupil's name.

2 Do convey empathy by:

- reflecting feelings
- appropriate self-disclosure: 'I had an experience like that. I found it disturbing'.

3 Do convey real feelings by:

- showing warmth – smile
- showing consideration
- showing consistency between verbal and non-verbal behaviour.

4 Don't:

- Show boredom, impatience, sigh, condescend or patronise.
- Look away, or check your watch.
- Play with pencils, keys, do anything that distracts or shows inattention.
- Devalue or negate by:

    minimising – 'Everyone has problems'
    over caring – 'I'm sure you wouldn't do anything silly'
    disbelieving – 'I don't think you mean that'.

- Jump to conclusions – this can eliminate helpful options.
- Pass judgment – if you are counselling, you must not evaluate.
- Jump in – wait for a non-verbal invitation.
- Interrupt – your job is to listen and share your pupil's experience.
- Ask closed questions – they won't help to get a clear picture.
- Ask multiple questions – keep it simple.
- Accept generalisations, vagueness or evaluations – seek clarification.
- Mumble, ramble, use jargon or unfamiliar words – be clear.
- Give advice – you will not empathise.

Making up for lost time

The history of art is the history of revivals
(Samuel Butler, Handel and Music: Anachronism*)*

- When childhood illnesses, family holidays, other problems and lack of success set pupils back they will need help to make up lost ground.

- Once you have been informed of a planned absence – help pupils to set targets to minimise losses.

- When pupils return from illness for example, help them to set targets for recovery.

- Use targets, handouts, worksheets and differentiated materials as a recovery pack.

- Encourage pupils to assist their own recovery by asking questions about anything they don't understand (see *Encouraging Pupils to Talk*, page 88).

- Use pair and small group work to assist recovery and help other pupils to improve their communication skills.

- Encourage pupils to keep as up to date as possible while they achieve their targets for recovery.

- Encourage pupils who have missed lessons to keep cool, assess their problem calmly and follow an agreed plan.

- Help pupils to monitor their progress to assist recovery.

- Time lost through failure can be recovered more economically if pupils can be helped to react positively. Why did the pupil not succeed? What needs to be done to be successful?

- Show pupils how failure may be an indication that their learning and/or revision techniques need to be improved.

Progress through IT

Vorsprung durch Technik
(Advertising slogan for Audi cars, 1986)

Pupils learn in a variety of ways at different speeds. IT can help effective classroom managers to support individual pupils in different ways.

- IT allows pupils to work at their own pace, retrace learning steps and seek clarification.
- Computer software is patient and non-judgmental.
- IT can help a pupil to overcome physical disabilities by providing access to a wider curriculum.
- The novelty of IT can motivate pupils who have not enjoyed learning by:

  presenting information in an interesting manner
  giving them control
  producing attractive work
  providing regular, supportive feedback
  the privacy to make mistakes no one else will see.

- IT can help pupils to overcome a lack of basic skills and make progress.
- Spell-checkers enable pupils to improve the accuracy of their writing.
- A thesaurus can help pupils to use a wider vocabulary.
- Computer-aided design packages can help pupils who cannot draw well.
- IT can help pupils with emotional or behavioural problems to overcome low self-esteem and experience success.

FE, HE, job or career

The pleasantness of an employment does not always evince its propriety
(Jane Austen, Sense and Sensibility)

- Form tutors and subject teachers can supplement the formal guidance offered to pupils by careers advisers.
- Invite past pupils to participate in careers workshops.
- Arrange visits to FE and HE open days to provide pupils with further information about continuing education.
- Encourage pupils to prepare a Curriculum Vitae. Arrange for local employers, FE and HE colleagues to provide feedback on the ways that their CV may be received by employers and admission tutors.
- Arrange for the local Chamber of Commerce to speak to pupils about the 'window dressing' which looks good on an application.
- Help pupils to perform a strengths and weaknesses audit of skills, experience, qualifications and other attributes.
- Encourage pupils to role-play interviews.
- Ensure that pupils understand the impact of dress and body language.
- Encourage small groups of pupils to research the process of employment through job specifications, advertisements and applications.
- Invite employers to provide pupils with interview experience and give feedback on their performance.
- Invite employers to join interview case-study workshops.

Chapter 5

Some other things a teacher does

... it did lots of other things too

(James Joyce)

Teachers are performers. They act on a small stage. Their usual audience is small, streetwise and highly critical. Like all stand-up acts, a classroom performer's planning, preparation and timing are vital.

When the effective classroom manager moves outside of their classroom, where the audience may be larger, prejudiced and hypercritical, planning, preparation, timing and vigilance are essential elements in the professional support system.

Effective planning and preparation create a structure and purpose for teaching, learning and reporting – moving the National Curriculum, examination syllabuses, parental, pupil, community and institutional expectations from ideology into action.

Timing and vigilance ensure that the effective classroom manager is never caught off balance. During parental consultations, on school trips and in other teachers' classrooms balance and diplomacy are essential.

Parents' evenings

Parents should conduct their arguments in quiet, respectful tones...
(Judith Martin, Advice from Miss Manners' Column in the
Washington Post)

- Before a parents' consultation make appointments at ten minute intervals. On the day confirm who will be attending.

- Discuss with each pupil his or her Record of Achievement. Agree strengths and weakness, successes and failures. Make notes, prepare a short script to ensure that you can present a clear picture of each pupil's achievements and needs.

- Make sure that you can identify each pupil – copies of individual/form photographs are invaluable. Agree the name to be used when talking to parents – Thomas not Tom.

- Collect a folio of work to underline your assessment and comments.

- Tell parents you will make notes for target setting and feedback.

- Identify yourself with a clearly visible name plate. Introduce yourself, make it clear that you are talking about **Name**.

- Relate a pupil's achievements to benchmarks, not to other pupils.

- Avoid comparisons with siblings.

- Comment on National Curriculum performance, contributions to the whole class and extra curricular activities – not personality.

- The subject for discussion with each set of parents is their child's performance. Refer other matters to the Headteacher.

- Ensure that you have drinks and high energy food available – mineral water, flapjacks and bananas are excellent emergency rations.

- Telephone those parents who were unable to attend the consultation.

ECM

Handling problem parents

Because of their size, parents may be difficult to discipline properly (P.J. O'Rourke, Modern Manners)

Avoid confrontation.

Headteachers and senior members of staff have the experience and status to handle problem parents.

- Parents do not have a right of access to individual teachers.

- Whenever possible refer complainants to the Headteacher, your Head of Department, or a senior member of staff.

- If you have made a mistake, explain it to your Head of Department, or Headteacher. They can resolve the issue according to school policy.

- Do not remain alone in a classroom with complaining parents. Carefully move into a public area.

- Reduce tension by listening. Show parents that you want to understand their concerns.

- Don't raise your voice. Quietly tell parents what has happened. A cool, calm demeanour can catch on.

- Explain the action/reaction which has caused the problem. Avoid any reference to personalities.

- Show parents that you understand what they are saying. Without patronising them restate their case. Explain that you can see their point of view, but cannot agree with it.

- Provide an opportunity for parents to withdraw and save face.

- When the problem has been resolved, ensure that parents and pupil(s) understand that the matter is closed and will not affect future relations.

Avoid confrontation.

Accidents and emergencies

Accidents will occur in the best-regulated families
(Charles Dickens, David Copperfield)

- Don't panic! Pupils will learn to keep calm if you do.

- Take risk assessments seriously – be aware of what could happen in your classroom and playground.

- Learn First Aid.

- If a pupil is injured, or seriously ill, send two reliable pupils to get help.

- Talk to pupils as you work. This will help you to assess the situation and focus on what needs to be done.

- Move walking wounded to a peaceful place. If necessary create a quiet corner in the classroom.

- You may not get it right first time. Learn from your experience. You can role-play emergencies during INSET.

- Create an emergency file based on risk assessments and case studies. Include *how to routines* for specific events such as electrocution, falls and wounds.

- After the event talk through what happened. A debrief for you will help you to be even better should you face another emergency.

- Don't panic!

Working with others

From each according to his abilities, to each according to his needs (Karl Marx, Criticism of the Gotha Programme)

Teachers no longer work on their own in one classroom. The National Curriculum and other initiatives have made working together part of school life. Collaboration can create an inclusive school spirit. The benefits can be realised by all members of the school community.

- Collaboration can make the good times bad and the bad times better.
- Planning together increases individual and group efficiency.
- Working groups can produce better teaching and learning materials.
- Sharing information draws part-time and temporary staff into the group.
- Plan collaborative work so that the group and individual members know who will be responsible for particular aspects of the enterprise.
- Tell colleagues what you are doing. Annotate your short term plans so that cover teachers can be more easily briefed.
- Present a united front to parents and pupils. If you have a case to argue – do it professionally and privately.
- Deadlines are not the moment to start negotiating. Collaborative work requires confidence and trust. Meet agreed targets, or go back to the group to discuss rearrangements in good time.
- Be punctual and well prepared for meetings.
- Encourage sharing by offering your resources and skills to others.
- Encourage colleagues to share by asking them for advice and support.
- Agree performance indicators for collaborative work – use them for regular reviews.

Covering for absent colleagues

*... when they are away, we console ourselves for their absence by
dwelling on their vices
(George Bernard Shaw,* Heartbreak House)

In-house cover for absent colleagues is easier than supply cover as
the teachers are on familiar ground. Supply cover requires flexible,
reliable, strong teachers to maintain stability and standards in the
classroom.

- If possible, discuss a cover lesson in advance. Make sure
  that you know what you have to do, what the pupils are
  expected to achieve and where resources will be. Ask for
  a copy of the short term plan.

- Build up a file of crosswords, wordsearches or worksheets
  for all ages and abilities, to plug the gaps when there is
  insufficient work for pupils to do.

- Take paper, pencils, pens into the classroom as exercise
  books and so on may not be available at short notice.

- Draw a quick classroom plan, add names (see *Allow their
  names to be mentioned,* page 19) as you take the register.
  If there isn't a register – count heads and check names as
  you move around the classroom.

- Be firm but fair. Explain the learning objectives to be
  achieved. Emphasise the time available to complete the
  planned work.

- Don't criticise the work the pupils are doing or have done.

- Don't discuss the school or staff (see *Supply Teachers' Code
  of Conduct,* page 103).

- Don't be sidetracked. Follow the activities set out in the
  lesson plan, help pupils achieve their learning objectives
  (see *Short Term Planning,* page 44).

- At the end of the lesson replace all resources. Make sure
  that the classroom is tidy and all pupils have left the room.

Supply teachers' Code of Conduct

For many of our pupils teachers provide the stability which they lack at home. Your task, as a supply teacher, is to maintain that stability when a class or subject teacher is absent.

We expect learning to be encouraged and discipline to be maintained in accordance with school policies (see *Supply Teachers' Handbook*). We expect supply teachers to be flexible, reliable colleagues who can contribute to school life.

The senior management team, heads of department and staff will provide material and professional support to help you realise these expectations. Your named senior manager is **Name**.

- We expect staff to be appropriately dressed for their contracted work.
- We expect supply teachers new to the school to provide identification such as a driving licence or passport.
- **Name** will provide an identification badge containing photograph.
- It is inadvisable to take valuable possessions into classrooms. Please leave valuable items at the school office and obtain a receipt.
- Please arrive at school by 08.30.
- When you arrive at school please contact your senior manager.
- **Name** will provide you with a printed programme for the day and a plan of the school.
- Please do not touch a pupil for any reason.
- Please do not leave a classroom unnecessarily.
- Never leave young pupils unattended for any reason, or allow them to leave a classroom early at the end of the day.
- Classroom Assistants are occasionally available to support you, but you are responsible for the class.
- If you have an accident which results in injury, it must be entered into the School Accident Book.
- At the end of the day please return your badge and work schedule to the school office.

Thank you for your cooperation. We hope that you will enjoy working with us.

School trips and visits

*There are two classes of travel – first class, and with children
(Robert Benchley, Pluck and Luck)*

Trips and visits have an important part to play in school life as part of the curriculum and as extra curricular activities. They are a awesome responsibility and require meticulous planning.

- Follow school and LEA guidelines for educational visits.
- Obtain approval from your headteacher or governors.
- Send parents a written outline of the visit. Obtain signed parental permissions, make photocopies, place originals in your school safe.
- Hold a briefing for parents and pupils. Provide a complete itinerary, with emergency telephone contacts, times and safe places for regrouping.
- Explain expected standards of behaviour to everyone.
- Produce a timed visit plan – busy pupils behave better.
- A safe school trip does not include free time.
- Provide a kit list: clothes, money, food and drink. Pack a spare kit bag – everything that others might forget.
- Include a trained first aider in your staff/parent team.
- Wear something very visible.
- Plan back at school activities.
- Count pupils, count them again, and again.

School Visit Checklist

	CATEGORY OF VISIT		
	A	B	C
This basic information should be provided and discussed with the Head (who will need to seek approval from the Governing Body for hazardous category C visits)			
1 Purpose of visit			
2 Educational objectives of the visit			
3 Full details of the proposed visit including any special circumstances or activities and nature of accommodation	███████		
4 Nature of any hazardous activities			
5 Place(s) which it is proposed to visit, with existing knowledge of them in school and whether a preliminary visit is planned			
6 Transport arrangements			
7 Name/address(es) and telephone number of accommodation to be used or places to be visited.			
8 Costings and financial arrangements			
9 Details of any organising agency/company to be used	████		
10 Dates and times of visit(s)/journey(s) – leaving – activities – returning			
11 Headteacher/governing body consent			
12 Information for parents and consent form			
13 Number of school days involved	███████		
14 Planned size and composition of the party, including the age range of pupils			
15 Name(s) and relevant experience of party leader(s) and deputies			
16 Number, names and relevant qualifications (including first aid) of school staff in party.			
17 Number, names and relevant specialist qualifications of other adults in party			
18 Details of insurance			
19 Plans for pupils remaining in school			
20 Staff briefing			
21 Parent briefing			
22 Pupil briefing			
23 Registration and reporting back procedures.			
24 Private cars insured for business/educational visits			

School Visit Staff/Pupil Information Sheet

SCHOOL/COLLEGE			
Visit to	No of pupils	Female	Male
Name & phone number of link person			
PLEASE PRINT			
NAMES OF STAFF AND PUPILS	HOME ADDRESS	TEL NO	MEDICAL INFO
1 DARREN MAJOR	12 ANY STREET, OURTOWN, ON12 3XZ	123987	ASTHMA
2			
3			
4			
5			
6			
7			
8			
9			
10			
TEACHER IN CHARGE		DATE	

Parental consent form

(Category A & B visits)

School: ....

1 *Details of journey/visit to:* ....

 ....

 From ....*Date/Time To* ....*Date/Time*

 I agree to my daughter/son...*(name)*

 taking part in the above-mentioned visit and, having read the information sheet, agree to her/his participation in any or all activities described. I acknowledge the need for obedience and responsible behaviour on her/his part.

2 *Declaration*

 I understand that while the adults in charge of the party will take all reasonable care of the young people, they cannot necessarily be held responsible for any loss, damage or injury suffered or as a result of the journey/visit.

Signature of parent/guardian: ....

Date: ....

Parental consent form

(Category C visits)

School: ....

1   *Details of journey/visit to:* ....

    ....

    From ....*Date/Time To* ....*Date/Time*

    I agree to my daughter/son...*(name)*

    taking part in the above-mentioned visit and, having read the
    information sheet, agree to her/his participation in any or all
    activities described. I acknowledge the need for obedience and
    responsible behaviour on her/his part.

2   *Medical Information*

    (a) *Does your daughter/son suffer from any conditions requiring
        medical treatment, including medication?*

        If YES, please give brief details..

        ....

        ....

    (b) *To the best of your knowledge, has your daughter/son been in
        contact with any contagious or infectious diseases or suffered
        from anything in the last four weeks that may be or become
        contagious or infectious?*

        If YES, please give brief details..

        ....

        ....

        ....

    (c) *Is your daughter/son allergic to any medication?*

        If YES, please give brief details

        ....

        ....

    (d) *Has your daughter/son received a tetanus injection in the last
        five years?*
        YES/NO

Please outline any special dietary requirements of your child.

I undertake to inform the head as soon as possible of any change in the medical circumstances between the date signed and the commencement of the journey.

3 **Declaration**

I understand that while the adults in charge of the party will take all reasonable care of the young people, they cannot necessarily be held responsible for any loss, damage or injury suffered arising as a result of the journey/visit.

I agree to my daughter/son receiving emergency medical treatment, including anaesthetic, as considered necessary by the medical authorities present. I understand the extent and limitations of the insurance cover provided.

I may be contacted by telephone on the following numbers:

Work: ....

Home: ....

Mobile: ....

If not available at any of the above, please contact:

Name: ....

Telephone number: ....

Address: ....

Name, address and telephone number of family doctor:

..

..

..

Date: ....Signed: ....

I understand that the cost of the visit will be.................................

to be paid in full by ....

Signature of parent/guardian: ....

Date...

This form or a copy must be taken by the leader on the activity. During holidays a copy should be retained by the responsible authority.

School visit sample letter to parents

Date

Dear Parent/Guardian

We are hoping to take the pupils of 8ZX to see a theatre production of The Witches by Roald Dahl at the Theatre Royal in Ourtown. This will be a matinee performance at 2.00 pm on Thursday February 25th 1998. We intend to travel to the City Centre by service bus, leaving Any Street at approximately 1.00 pm. Early dinners will be available if required.

The performance will end after normal school hours and we would request that parents make their own arrangements for the collection of their children from the Theatre Royal. We shall inform you of the finishing time nearer the date. If this presents any problem please contact us at the school.

The trip will cost £4.25 per pupil, inclusive of the theatre ticket and bus fare to the theatre. In accordance with DfEE regulations (Circular No 1234) we are required to inform you of Government Policy. As the trip is to take place mainly in school hours, it must be funded by voluntary contributions from pupils. "There is no obligation to contribute and no pupil would be omitted from the activity because her or his parents were unwilling or unable to contribute." However, the trip would not go ahead without your financial support.

The pupils of 8ZX are currently reading The Witches in their English lessons so it will be a valuable educational experience for them to see an adaption of the text. Please return the reply slip with the money if you would like your daughter/son to attend the performance.

Yours faithfully

J Soap

....*tearoff*..

I would like my daughter/son ....to visit the Theatre Royal on February 25th. I have read and agree to abide by the conditions in the letter dated 9th February 1998. I enclose the trip money of £4.25.

Signature of parent/guardian:...

School visits – the legal position

In Loco Parentis

The term 'in loco parentis' is used to describe the responsibility of a teacher towards the pupil. Literally, it means 'in the place of a parent'. Whilst a child is in a teacher's care, some of the privileges of the natural parent are transferred to the teacher so that they may carry out their duties. In return, the teacher must assume certain responsibilities and recognise that both legal and moral obligations rest upon them in every aspect of their work.

The degree of care required, of course, depends to a considerable extent upon the age of the pupil and, indeed, to some extent upon the particular susceptibilities of the individual pupil which ought to be known to the teacher. Older pupils may self-evidently be exposed reasonably to greater risk than younger pupils. However, the duty of care is not extinguished simply because the pupil has attained the adult age of 18. At that age the pupil may, of course, reasonably be expected to behave as an adult but there remains upon the teacher the duty of care to instruct and impart knowledge with reasonable foresight of the consequences.

Implications for Leaders

By law all teachers have a **common duty of care** towards their pupils of whatever age. This means that a teacher must take such care of her/his pupils as a prudent parent would take.

Improving listening skills

If one could only teach the English how to talk, and the Irish how to listen, society here would be quite civilised
(Oscar Wilde, An Ideal Husband)

1 **Eye contact** is the most important way of communicating full and undivided attention.

- Focus your eyes on the other person;
- Don't stare or feign eye contact;
- Avoid looking away for long periods.

2 **Non-verbal prompts**, such as:

- occasional affirmative head nodding paired with good eye contact;
- appropriate facial expressions reflecting the speaker's feelings;
- a relaxed open body posture, show that you are listening.

3 **A frown** is appropriate when you don't understand the speaker's point.

4 **Silence** shows that you are a patient listener.

5 **Verbal prompts** can encourage someone to keep talking.

- Ask open questions: 'How do you feel about ...?'
- Summarising gives you an opportunity to check that you have really heard, and allows the speaker to review what he has said.
- Ask for specific examples.
- Point out discrepancies.

6 **Move away from furniture** which can be both a psychological and physical barrier.

Using a video

Watch and pray, that ye enter not into temptation
(St Matthew, 26:41)

- Don't be tempted to use watching television, or a video, as a crowd pleaser.

- Most pupils will have a VCR at home. Avoid a major loss of street cred – know how to operate all of the school VCRs.

- Watch the video before the lesson. If you intend stopping and moving on, make a note of the counter readings. Be sure to start at zero.

- Try the video in the viewing area.

    Will all pupils be able to see the screen?
    Is the blackout adequate at all times of day?

- Explain why you are using the video.

    Explain the benefits of video over other media.
    Don't just watch and move on.
    Tie the video into your learning objectives.

- Increase concentration with questions to be answered, or a programme based activity.

- 'How long will the show be?'
    Pupils will have very different concentration spans so plan accordingly.

- Ensure that pupils grasp the main issues – pause, ask questions, review or forecast.

Invigilating examinations

The condition on which God hath given liberty to man is eternal vigilance
(John Philpot Curran, On the election of the Lord Mayor of Dublin, 1790)

- Provide a secure place for pupils to leave their belongings.

- Tell pupils that they should not take any prohibited materials into the examination room – they will need to check their pockets and pencil cases.

- Ensure a prompt start to the examination.

- Provide time checks, but do not create extra stress.

- Be vigilant.
  See as much as you can without being seen.

- Quietly and unobtrusively walk around the examination room handing out extra writing paper.

- Maintain an accurate seating plan. This can corroborate or dismiss suspicions of collaboration.

- If you suspect cheating make a timed note of the event.

- For external examinations read the examination board's regulations beforehand and follow them.

- Make special arrangements for pupils who suffer from stress.

- Be sympathetic at all times.

Getting ready for an inspection

*Now, what I want is facts... Facts alone are wanted in life
(Charles Dickens, Mr Gradgrind: Hard Times)*

- Develop stress management strategies now!
- Read the Ofsted *Handbook for the Inspection of Schools*.
- Read whole school, department and phase policies – collect evidence to show that you follow them.
- Be well prepared.
- Always state your learning objectives clearly.
- Show how schemes of work, lesson plans, teaching and pupils' learning are compatible with the National Curriculum Programmes of Study and examination board syllabuses.
- Show how and when teaching and learning are assessed.
- Show how you differentiate to meet individual needs, and that you teach lessons for a range of abilities and learning experiences.
- Have adequate resources available and accessible.
- Show how you cover cross-curricular themes.
- Don't panic!
- Continue to teach effective lessons.

Using a library

Th' first thing to have in a libry is a shelf. Fr'm time to time this can be decorated with lithrachure. But th' shelf is th' main thing.
(Finley Peter Dunne, Mr Dooley Says)

- Libraries can be intimidating if pupils have not used them as family readers. Train your pupils to use the classroom library/resource area as a first step towards school and public libraries.

- Introduce pupils to the catalogue or index through exciting reference searches. Remember, there is now CD-Rom as well as Dewey Decimal.

- Encourage pupils to develop real searching skills by focusing on relevant tasks. At first tell them what to look for and where to look (see *Treasure Island*, page 117)

- Build on basic search skills through group and individual library tasks (see *The Clothes Show*, page 118).

- Encourage pupils to ask librarians for help. Arrange for a public or university librarian to talk to pupils, then visit the library and see it in action.

- Emphasise that good researchers read the contents page and index first – it saves time.

- Show pupils how to make useful notes.

- Train pupils to acknowledge sources and refer to them accurately.

Treasure Island worksheet

Use a dictionary and the dictionary of word origins to find the:
- part of speech
- meaning
- origin

of the following words

blunderbus

buccaneer

captain

cutlass

gallows

mutiny

pirate

treachery

treasure

victim

The Clothes Show worksheet

Imagine that television had been invented at the time Tennyson wrote *The Charge of the Light Brigade* and the impact of the Crimean War on clothing was the first subject of a Clothes Show Special.

As a first step towards writing your script, use the school library to answer the following questions.

- **Where is The Crimea?**

  World Index, Atlas

- **What is the winter weather like in Crimea?**

  CD-Rom encyclopedia

- **Where is Balaclava?**

  World Index, Atlas

- **What is a Balaclava?**

  Dictionary

- **What is the connection between James Thomas Brudenell and the cardigan?**

  Dictionary of Word Origins

- **Why did Lord Raglan, the British Commander-in-Chief in the Crimean War, need an overcoat without shoulder seams?**

  Dictionary

ECM

Stock control

Let all things be done decently and in order
(Corinthians, 14:40)

- Save time by storing everyday resources in clearly labelled places so that pupils have easy access.
- Keep pens and pencils in drilled wooden blocks of ten – allowing a quick visual check for missing items.
- Use clearly labelled 'free' storage such as shoe boxes and plastic tubs to keep small items in a safe place.
- Collect drafting/working out paper from 'free' sources such as computer printouts.
- Keep breakable/valuable items in a restricted store and ensure that pupils understand that they must log them out and back in.
- Make sure pupils understand that even 'free' resources have a cost such as the time taken to collect them.
- Keep extension material in a clearly labelled place.
- Ensure that pupils tidy resources away after use.
- Ensure that consumables are always available.
- Encourage ownership and responsibility by involving pupils in daily/weekly resource management.

Managing limited resources

There is, however, a limit at which forbearance ceases to be a virtue (Edmund Burke, Observations on 'The Present State of the Nation'*)*

- Ensure that colleagues, parents and pupils understand that budgets are finite, not elastic.
- Count everything out and everything in.
- Encourage all pupils to own and care for resources.
- Recycle everything you can.
- Use your IT skills and equipment to produce in-house resources designed to meet your pupils' needs rather than buy expensive branded goods.
- Issue a termly shopping list of 'free' resources.
- Encourage donation through sponsored resources.
- Ask business associations, companies and publishers for educational material. (Read everything carefully before using it in the classroom.)
- Ask local colleges, companies and newspapers for visits which allow you to use their resources.
- Find out what is available locally. The *Hull Daily Mail* funds a community classroom equipped with Apple Macs.

ECM

Creating an attractive learning environment

C-l-e-a-n, clean, verb active, to make bright, to scour. W-i-n, win, d-e-r, der, winder, a casement. When the boy knows this is out of a book, he goes and does it.
(Charles Dickens, Nicholas Nickleby)

- It's your classroom. Mark out your territory with non-exclusive displays.

- Make a virtue out of necessity, cover peeling paintwork with attractive posters.

- Stimulate interest with subject specific material. If your teaching modern languages, make sure everyone knows!

- Display interesting artifacts.

- Create a class/subject library – use eye-catching books to attract attention.

- Display pupils' work.

- Encourage care, ownership and responsibility by asking pupils to contribute items for display.

- Set up a CEEFAX or WEBSITE on your computer.

- Encourage care and responsibility by asking pupils to produce a weekly maintenance schedule.

- Arrange the classroom furniture to maximise learning opportunities and minimise disruption.

Distinctive displays

Now it is the virtue of design
(Gerard Manley Hopkins, Letter to Robert Bridges)

- Show and tell – visitors to both primary and secondary schools should be able to tell what has been happening in the classrooms by the show of pupils' work.

- Mark your territory – visitors to secondary classrooms should be immediately aware of subject specialism from displays of artifacts, posters and work.

- Multi-media has more impact – use black and white, colour, photographs, pictures, the written word and textured materials.

- Mount pupils' work to achieve maximum impact. (See *North Ferriby CE Primary School Display Policy,* page 123).

- Provide a context for understanding – briefly explain, in writing, what the display is about.

- Involve pupils in creating displays and create a greater feeling of ownership. Teach presentation skills and draw on prior learning for maximum impact.

- Use cool, crisp lettering – computer generated sans serif fonts such as Helvetica and Lucida Bright are ideal.

- Choose a dark background to make work stand out.

- Double mount, or draw a Mondrian style black border around white/light paper.

- Don't leave displays to get tatty – keep them fresh.

North Ferriby CE Primary School display policy

Name of School	North Ferriby CE Primary
Date of Policy	Presented September 1995
Reviewed	September 1996
Next Review	September 1997
Co-ordinator	Head

Policy Formation

1 The Head and teaching staff met and agreed the need to develop a specific policy on display.

2 An audit was made by Head or present practice.

3 All teaching staff were involved in setting up guidelines.

4 Consultation then took place with other members of staff.

Aims

North Ferriby CE Primary School believes that the display should reflect the very ethos of the school and influence the learning environment in which we all work. It should be an integral part of the curriculum delivered and an important part of the planning across all areas.

Objectives

i)   to create a visually stimulating rich learning environment.

ii) to arouse curiosity.

iii) to foster participation and interaction.

iv) to stimulate enquiry.

v)   to encourage, praise and enhance efforts/achievements of all children.

vi) to communicate useful and relevant information.

vii) to present materials well – as a model of excellent example and to act as a challenge to extend the quality of children's work.

Basic Guidelines

1   <u>Backing Paper</u>

Colourplan large sheets of quality paper in muted shades. Neutral colours make the best background for children's work. Remember bright colours will only distract the eye from the children's work. Backing paper and display mounts should enhance the work on display.

Colourplan is found in the library in the main school or in the hall of the new building. The paper does not have to be brand new but must be clean and uncreased. Indeed the used colourplan is replaced back on top of the cupboard in order that it can be re-used. Colourplan used for backing of the pin boards may be stapled with the gun stapler to make secure.

Efforts should be made to form a subtle contrast between the mount and the children's work to provide a balance.

2   Avoid clutter. Very often the best effective displays are simple.

3   Large display areas (formerly thought of as frieze (sp) boards look better if broken up into smaller areas using strips/ colours with different types of work.

4   Don't put work at odd angles.

5   Avoid 'things' hanging off the edge of the display board.

6   Always title and label the display. Provide contextual information and use interactive labels. This helps children (and adults) to focus on the work rather than just looking at it as decorative.

7   <u>Mounting</u>

All work to be displayed for any length of time is to be thoughtfully mounted.

i) <u>Single Mounting</u>

Well trimmed work, mounted on a contrasting background – dark on light/light on dark.

ii) <u>Double Mounting</u>

This is well worth the extra effort. The initial piece of work is mounted first onto a contrasting background which in turn is mounted onto a second background. It usually looks better to make the inner frame thinner with a broader outer frame.

Strip mounting can help with the economics, or alternatively commercially prepared A4 mounts and double mounts can be purchased. These can be used again and again.

iii) <u>Window Mounting</u>

A frame is made out of card with mitred corners e.g. a picture frame.

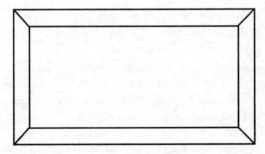

Children need to learn how to best display their own work from an early stage in order that when they are in Key Stage II they can "choose" how to display.

The time and effort needed to prepare a stimulating and aesthetic display not to mention energy is acknowledged, however, any display whatever quality takes time.

The impact of an attractive well thought out and stimulating display can have an enormous impact on the learning environment and our children deserve the best.

Further guidelines to consider:-

- The use of pinking shears can seem attractive but can also make work look gimmicky and unfinished.
- Care should be taken to avoid overlapping and visible use of sellotape.
- No drawing pins to be used, they detract from the child's work. Instead use mapping pins – try to co-ordinate colour.
- Straight pins may be used if above childrens eye level (remember to inset at an angle).
- A drape may not always be appropriate, if used it should be clean and pressed. Design, texture and colour should enhance the display not detract from the work. (See appendix 1.)
- Use of wooden templates, computer print out or handwritten are all acceptable lettering but must reflect the handwriting style of the school and be clear and well written.
- Consider the height of the display. As the majority of display is aimed at children they must be able to see so it has to be at their eye level.
- Alphabets, time lines, number lines need to be within touching reach of younger children. This can often be difficult and sometimes the tendency is to put it high to avoid or place over door ways etc. The design of our classrooms does not lend itself to long unbroken lines. Do please take the time to look at all display from your children's view point.

Displays can vary in their objectives:-

i) The majority of displays are about celebrating children's work. The message we are hoping to give is one of valuing and respecting. It should not long be representative of the best work in the class but samples of individual's special efforts.

ii) <u>Interactive Displays</u>

Most displays can fall into this category by asking open questions but some displays can be deliberately asking children to touch, examine and feel. Topic display – often examples to which children have contributed e.g. electricity, magnets.

iii) <u>Stimulus for learning</u>

This display is often set up as a "launching point" for some area of learning and is intended to provoke discussion through excitement and challenge to develop an immediate interest.

iv) Display of material and equipment in order to inform as to resources available.

Obviously some displays can incorporate more than one objective but as the creator of the display it is important that you are clear in your mind exactly what you are hoping the children will achieve and gain from it.

Displays in classrooms should reflect work which is happening at that time in the classroom. This work can later be used for corridor or hall display to share with the rest of the school. Displays are not expected to change every week. This is neither necessary nor desirable. But please ensure a display is never left to become dusty, dirty, untidy or "unlooked at". It may not be necessary to completely change a display, just rotating children's work with the addition/removal of alternative items can be enough to keep the interest.

We want the children to experience high standards and enjoy a quality environment. As the majority of the curriculum is delivered through 1/2 termly sessions, six weeks would be a good length of time for a particular display.

Practicalities of achieving an aesthetic Display

Points to consider:-

1   Have an overall vision and clear objective as to what you are trying to achieve.

2   Arrange on a table or floor first in order to achieve balance.

3   Think about the colour of background and put in place. Secure with a tacker as our pin boards are well used and worn down at the corners! Place work with 1 pin (this leaves it much easier to reposition).

4   Consider the space in front of the display. Do you need a table for 3D work? Different heights? Do you need covered boxes? Table tops and additionally boxes need covering. A drape may be appropriate to link paper, boxes and children's work together.

Chapter 6

Working with colleagues

No man is an Island, entire of itself; every man is a piece of the Continent, a part of the main

(John Donne, Devotions)

The days when a teacher could close their classroom door after morning assembly and only open it for playtime, lunchtime and hometime are, thankfully, long gone. Teachers are members of a team, or teams.

As a member of a team, the effective classroom manager will be committed to a common purpose. They will respect their colleagues and accept whatever team function or role is necessary.

To promote good relations and open communications the effective classroom managers will express themselves openly and honestly. They will listen actively to colleagues and value their different perspectives.

Staff meetings

Our stern alarums changed to merry meetings
(Shakespeare, Richard III*)*

- Staff meetings have two positive purposes – to disseminate information and discuss policy.

- They can also be used negatively to air individual problems or group gripes. It is vital for staff morale that these meetings do not create a complaint culture.

- The Headteacher or Chair of the meeting should provide an agenda.

- Comments should be addressed to the chair in order to promote an efficient exchange of views.

- The meeting can be more efficient if certain regular agenda items are timed – a five minute report back on discipline or homework.

- The meeting should have an agreed closing time.

- Discussion papers should be tabled at least 48 hours before the meeting.

- The first staff meeting of a new school year will need to cover a wide range of topics and information – help it to progress.

- New members of staff can expect to be introduced at a staff meeting, so prepare a short aide memoire to ensure that you say what you want and make a positive impression.

- Always make notes so that you can:

    carry out agreed tasks and instructions
    check out the accuracy of the minutes.

- For new members of staff, these meetings are like cricket. It is unwise to attempt any fancy strokes until you have 'played yourself in'.

Managing senior staff

*I understand. You work very hard two days a week and you need a
five-day weekend. That's normal.*
(Neil Simon, Come Blow Your Horn)

Effective senior managers manage themselves and the people
they work with so that both the institution and its staff achieve
their targets.

- Try to avoid problems with senior managers by adopting a
  positive attitude.

- A problem exists only if there is a difference between
  what is happening and what you want to happen. Anything
  else is grumbling.

- If you want to change something – look ahead. Present
  policy papers and make suggestions which will attract
  support.

- Before you present a paper to a staff meeting or
  committee try it out on people who will be there.
  Organise support and count votes in favour.

- If you have a difference of opinion, is it caused by policy or
  personality? It is vital to identify the behaviour you need to
  manage and adopt appropriate strategies.

- If the problem is personality you can keep contact to a
  professional minimum, or talk about the issue with
  colleagues. Agree a plan for mutual support.

- If the problem is policy, read new proposals carefully and
  work out how they might affect you. Offer a better
  proposal in an appropriate forum.

- Aggressions, bad temper, cynicism and sarcasm don't
  resolve difficulties. They are inappropriate behaviours, so
  avoid them – be cool.

- Ensure that all meetings are minuted. If decisions are taken which affect you, summarise what you think has been decided and invite other participants to agree.
- Keep accurate, dated, timed notes during any disagreement.
- Once a problem is resolved it is over. As John F. Kennedy said: 'Forgive your enemies. Just never forget their names!'

The role of the headteacher

The final test of a leader is that he leaves behind him in other men the conviction and will to carry on
(Walter Lippmann, New York Herald Tribune)

Headteachers should:

- provide leadership and have a clear view of where the school is going
- have an open mind, consultative style
- be constructive, enthusiastic and positive
- plan, train and evaluate to ensure the quality of the curriculum
- evaluate the standards of teaching and learning in the school
- show appreciation of the work done and results achieved by staff
- support staff in difficult situations
- manage the budget according to powers delegated by the governing body
- advise the governing body
- be well organised and in touch with events in the school
- help staff to prepare for change and monitor results
- maintain a high, non-threatening profile in the school and community
- delegate tasks, but not responsibility
- appoint, deploy and appraise staff
- ensure the maintenance of good order and discipline
- encourage good relations between the school and community
- avoid bandwagons and initiative overload.

The role of the governing body

The Government should take a firm, bold line
(Queen Victoria, Letter to Lord Beaconsfield)

Governing Bodies must:

- manage their school effectively
- provide a safe and caring teaching and learning environment
- decide how the budget is spent and publish annual accounts
- agree a curriculum statement ensuring that the National Curriculum and RE are taught and a daily act of collective worship takes place
- agree a policy on sex education
- ensure provision for pupils with special education needs
- be aware of employment, race relations and sex discrimination acts
- promote good industrial relations
- have disciplinary procedures from staff
- make arrangements for hearing staff grievances
- control and manage school premises
- encourage the local community to use school premises
- prepare admissions literature
- keep an attendance register
- produce an annual report to parents about the school budget, exam results, pupil achievement and school policies
- hold an annual parents' meeting to discuss the parents' report
- individual governors do not have the power to act alone
- the chair has limited powers to act alone on safety matters.

The role of the teachers' organisations

Had the employers of past generations all of them dealt fairly with their men there would have been no unions
(Stanley Baldwin, Speech in Birmingham, 1931)

1 Every employee has the right to join an independent trade union.

2 Unions can represent and protect their members during lawful industrial action concerned with:

- pay and conditions of employment
- appointment or termination of employment
- the allocation of work and job descriptions
- staff discipline
- negotiation
- some trade union matters.

3 Unions can provide legal and professional support to:

- defend a complaint from a parent or pupil
- pursue a case of unfair dismissal
- defend a complaint of serious misconduct
- complain about an employer's racial or sexual discrimination
- clarify the School Teachers' Pay and Conditions Document.

4 Most trade unions offer their members some of these services:

- free personal accident insurance
- free insurance of personal property on school premises
- free insurance against malicious damage to a vehicle on school premises
- competitive rates for life assurance, mortgages and personal insurance.

Teachers and the law

The one great principle of the English Law is, to make business for itself

(Charles Dickens, Bleak House)

1   An NQT in England and Wales will probably be employed in:

Type of school	Employer
LEA school with delegated Budget	LEA – most responsibilities for employment delegated to governors. (In voluntary-aided schools, the governors are employers.)
Grant-maintained	Governors.
City Technology College	Governors.
Sixth form, tertiary college	Governors.
Independent	Proprietor or governors.

In common with other employees a teacher is subject to the terms of a **contract of employment**. If you work for more than eight hours a week you must be provided with a statement of duties within two months of starting work.

2 Your contract of employment contains express and implied terms.

Express terms	Implied terms
Salary	May be general such as
Working hours	loyalty to employers, or
Pension contributions	a specific duty agreed at
Sick pay	your interview
Period of notice	

Your contract will refer to documents such as:

■ Teachers' Pay and Conditions Document (the Blue Book)

■ Conditions of Service for School Teachers in England and Wales (the Burgundy Book).

Express terms will always override implied terms if they are not 'unfair' or illegal.

3 If you are appointed on a fixed-term contract, usually for a year, you do not have the same rights as permanent employees. You may acquire rights under employment protection legislation. If you work for the same employer for two years you may have a right to a redundancy payment.

4 A teacher must carry out her professional duties under the reasonable direction of the head, or LEA if not attached to one school.

Teaching Duties
Planning and preparation
Teaching
Marking
Assessing
Recording & reporting progress

Hours and place of work

A full-time teacher has to be available for work on 195 days in any year.

She is required to teach pupils and carry out other duties on 190 of those days.

The other five non-teaching days are used at the head's discretion.

The maximum number of hours a teacher may be required to work as a teacher is 1265 which should be allocated reasonably throughout the year.

A teacher must be available to teach in the place specified by the head.

A teacher is required to work any additional hours that may be needed to enable her to fulfil her professional duties.

Other duties
Promoting progress & well-being
Providing guidance to pupils
Making records & reports about individual needs
Communicating & consulting with parents
Communicating & co-operating with outside agencies
Participating in meetings arranged for any of the above purposes
Participating in appraisal
Contributing to pupil assessments and references
Participating in professional development courses and training
Maintaining good order and school discipline
Safeguarding health & safety
Participating in curriculum, staff, administration, organisation and pastoral meetings
Teaching any pupil whose teacher is unavailable
Participating in arrangements for public examinations
Contributing to the selection of other teachers and non-teaching staff
Co-ordinating or managing the work of other teachers
Attending assemblies, registering the attendance of pupils
Supervising pupils before, during and after school sessions
Participating in administrative and management tasks related to all of the above duties.

5 Unexplained absence, poor time-keeping, insubordination, failure to prepare work, racial discrimination and sexual harassment can lead to **disciplinary proceedings** including dismissal.

Acceptable reasons with supporting evidence have to be given and the correct procedures have to be followed before a teacher can be disciplined or dismissed.

If an employer does not follow correct procedures there may be grounds for an appeal to an industrial tribunal or a judicial review by the high court.

Procedures for dismissal have to be fair. The Advisory, Conciliation and Arbitration Service (ACAS) has recommended this procedure:

- an informal oral warning – which may be recorded in a personal file
- a written warning
- a final warning
- dismissal.

You cannot be dismissed for belonging to a trade union, getting married, becoming pregnant, or on grounds of gender, religion or sexual orientation.

6 Following a **criminal conviction** a teacher can be dismissed, or the Secretary of State can declare her unfit to teach if there is sufficient evidence of gross misconduct – then her name is entered on List 99.

Misconduct does not mean an inability to teach. It usually refers to assault, fraud, multiple minor convictions, theft or sexual offenses.

7 Disciplinary action leading to dismissal can be taken against any teacher whose conduct is seen to be detrimental to the education and welfare of her pupils.

8 Most employers have introduced **sexual harassment policies**, which include disciplinary and dismissal procedures, to protect staff.

9 As well as the teaching and other duties detailed in 4 above, teachers have a **duty of care**. This is a legal and moral duty to ensure that their pupils are not harmed.

As teachers are acting in loco parentis, in place of the parent, the legal standard by which this duty is measured is how a reasonably careful and prudent parent might exercise care.

Under statute, common law and the school's Articles of Government a head has a responsibility to ensure that there is reliable and safe supervision of pupils whilst they are on school premises.

10 In loco parentis is a legal concept that governs everything a teacher does for, with an on behalf of her pupils.

A teacher must demonstrate that she is behaving, or has behaved, with the same degree of care and prudence as a reasonable parent.

The big question in relation to loco parentis is: *if I was the parent of this child would I believe that what I am doing is prudent and reasonable in the circumstances?*

A teacher may also consider:

- the nature of the activity or task
- dangers which a prudent and reasonable parent might anticipate
- the age and physical capacity of the pupils concerned, for example, it would be imprudent and unreasonable to take Key Stage 1 pupils on an assault course.
- the social and emotional context in which the activity will take place
- the physical environment in which the activity will take place
- specific safety routines which should be, for example, wearing safety glasses in a science laboratory or technology workshop
- the LEA and school procedures which must be followed.

11 Teachers are not required to supervise pupils during the midday break.

12 If a pupil has an accident you are not legally liable unless you have been **negligen**t. To demonstrate negligence an injured party has to show that you did not do something that you should have done.

A court will ask: *would a reasonable person have acted in this way in these circumstances?*

All schools keep formal records of accidents. If a pupil has an accident follow the school reporting procedures.

13 Schools have a statutory and common law duty to ensure that they are safe and healthy places in which to work. Every school should have a **health and safety policy**.

Health and safety legislation places a duty of care on all employers.

All employees must exercise reasonable care for their own and other people's health and safety.

14 It is vital that teachers take extra care of pupils when they are working in potentially **dangerous places** such as gymnasiums, laboratories and workshops, or on field trips.

Teachers have been found to be negligent when:

- a pupil was injured by an adult in a staff versus pupils rugby match because the teacher in charge failed to see the potential danger
- a pupil was burnt by sulphuric acid squirted by another pupil because the teacher failed to warn pupils of the danger
- a pupil was killed by a javelin during athletics training because there was inadequate supervision.

15 As part of their duty of care, all schools should provide clear guidance about the procedures to be used if staff suspect **child abuse** or **neglec**t.

16 Teachers should not **administer medicines** to pupils. Follow the school's guidelines. Never give pupils pain killers from your personal supply.

17 The content of the **school curriculum** will be set out in departmental and phase schemes of work. These will reflect the guidance given by the governing body, the LEA and school policies with due regard to the National Curriculum.

18 All maintained schools must teach **religious education** as part of the 5–18 curriculum. Each LEA will have an agreed syllabus which reflects mainly Christian traditions, with due regard to the teaching and practices of the other principal religions represented in our communities.

Teachers are not required to teach religious education or take part in collective worship – unless they work in voluntary aided church schools.

19 A school's governing body must decide, after consultation with the head, whether to teach **sex education** and what is to be taught. All sex education must reflect family life and moral values.

20 Section 44 of the Education (No. 2) Act 1986 forbids the 'pursuit of **political activities**' by any junior pupils and any promotion of partisan political views in the teaching of any subject to pupils in any school.

Section 45 requires the LEA, governors and head to take all reasonable steps to ensure that where political issues are brought to the attention of pupils, they are offered a balanced presentation of opposing views. This balance doesn't have to be provided in one lesson.

DES Circular 8/87 Annexe II recommends that, in order to protect pupils from political indoctrination and biased teaching, teachers should distinguish between fact and opinion, be ready to acknowledge personal bias, make clear that there may be different views legitimately held, and encourage pupils to form their own conclusions on the basis of evidence and reflection and discussion with others.

21 Teachers cannot be required to take part in **extra-curricular activities** unless directed by the head. Then a time allowance must be agreed.

22 Teachers have a contractual obligation to prepare, assess, **record** and **report** on a pupil's work. All maintained schools must report pupil progress to parents.

23 Governing bodies and LEAs should have policies and procedures for handling **complaints** about the curriculum and the assessment of pupils.

24 Under the Articles of Government headteachers are responsible for **discipline**. The Education (No. 2) Act 1986 states:

Teachers, too, have a duty under their conditions of employment to maintain good order and discipline.

25 Some schools punish pupils, others do not. It is a matter of ethos, policy and style. The last does not concern itself with the question of whether **punishment** should be used in schools.

Courts have made rulings on the use and abuse of punishment which have set limits on teachers' professional capacity to punish pupils.

■ All punishment must be reasonable and given in good faith. Any teacher who administered a harsh punishment out of proportion to the offense would probably not be acting reasonably or in good faith.

  Washing a pupil's mouth with soapy water as punishment for swearing would not be reasonable or in good faith.

■ The age, condition and other factors affecting the pupil must be borne in mind. An appropriate punishment for a 16-year-old secondary pupil could be inappropriate for a pupil in Key Stage 1.

■ Punishment should be in line with what the pupil's parents would expect. This presumes a normal, reasonable parent not given to excessive punishments in the home.

■ Any punishment must be such as is usual in the school. Punishments, if they are to be used, are usually detailed in a school's staff handbook and prospectus.

■ The 1986 Act banned **corporal punishment** in maintained schools.

■ The concept of in loco parentis allows teachers to place pupils in **detention** providing detention is a normal punishment used reasonably in the school - but parents can resume control of their children at any time. If, however, they are deemed to object to normal sanctions, the pupil may be suspended for not accepting the school's authority.

  Indiscriminate whole class detention which punishes all pupils for an individual's misbehaviour is not reasonable, nor is it in good faith.

■ A head can **exclude** a pupil either permanently or temporarily.

The LEA and governors have the power to direct a head to reinstate a pupil.

The Articles of Government will detail the local arrangements and procedures for appeals against exclusion.

26 The Education (No. 2) Act 1986 promoted partnership between school, governors, LEA and parents. The main provisions of the Act were designed to promote greater **parental participation** in school life and affairs:

- parents gained greater representation on governing bodies.
- an annual report to parents and an annual parents' meeting become statutory requirements.

Although governing bodies are required to provide an annual report to parents about their school, and hold an annual meeting for parents, teachers are not required to attend them.

27 Teachers do have an obligation to write **reports** and attend parents' consultation meetings to discuss pupils' progress. Any **record** kept by the school can be inspected by a pupil's parents.

ECM

Stress management

If you want to get somewhere else, you must run at least twice as fast as that!
(Lewis Carroll, Through the Looking Glass)

Some stress can be good for releasing hidden reserves of physical and creative energy. Too much stress causes anxiety, confusion and a lack of self-confidence, making it hard to complete tasks, make decisions or solve problems.

1 Stress management is a life skill:

- it cannot resolve all of the causes of stress
- it cannot make a demanding job easy
- it can cure self-induced stresses
- it can ease the effects of stress.

2 Managing stress requires an understanding of those situations which are most difficult to handle and those key factors which affect them.

- **Awareness** of a potentially stressful situation as it grows. It may help to keep a stress log for a week and record:

  date and time of stress

  details of the cause

  how you felt - did you suffer anxiety, irritable bowel or palpitations?

- **Identification** of warning signs which will help you to anticipate stressful situations in future.

- **Avoidance** of situations where stress cannot be contained.

- **Intervention** to defuse potentially stressful situations.

- **Assessment** of work and associated deadlines. It may be necessary to reassess priorities and learn to manage time more efficiently.

- **Asserting** your rights in a non-threatening way. Don't take on other people's burdens.
- **Action** to change work patterns and events which cause stress.

3 Visualise the way you will feel six weeks after making changes.

4 Adopt the motto: nothing in life matters very much, and most things don't matter at all.

Planning a career

Who controls the past... controls the future
(George Orwell, Nineteen Eighty-Four)

There is no promotion without application. Unless you are content to stay in one teaching post for the whole of your working life, you will need to manage your own career. You will need to apply your skills and energies to develop a career and obtain promoted posts.

■ There are five main strands to career development

become an expert teacher
get involved in extra-curricular activities
study for an MA in Education
become a good administrator
develop a reputation through In-service Education and
Training.

■ Develop your teaching skills by trying a variety of approaches. Keep a record of what works for you and what doesn't. Shadow successful colleagues to see how other teachers perform.

■ Collect a portfolio of evidence to promote your reputation in your own school and to support applications to other institutions.

■ Build on your personal interests and hobbies to make a significant contribution to the whole life of your school.

■ Extend your theoretical and applied knowledge of education through action research and study for an MA Ed. Publish the results of your work to extend your academic reputation.

■ Look for opportunities to acquire and sharpen administrative skills.

- Attend as many relevant courses as you can. As you develop your professional reputation look for opportunities to contribute to INSET.
- Read widely – be well informed on educational issues.
- Diplomatically and sensitively cultivate your reputation through networking in subject and professional associations.

ECM

Applying for jobs in teaching

Being a specialist is one thing, getting a job is another
(Stephen Leacock, The Boy I Left Behind Me)

- Use a word processor to create and maintain an up-to-date CV. This will enable you to act quickly if an interesting opportunity arises.

- Word process a generic letter of application which can be customised once you have read the specification for a particular job.

- Make all letters of application post and school specific.

- Spell check your CV and letter of application before you print it.

- Sense check your CV and letter of application, or get someone else to proof read it, before you post it.

- Photocopy the application form. Complete and check the copy before you start on the real form.

- Complete the form in your best handwriting. Make sure you use BLOCK CAPITALS when asked.

- Use blue or black ink.

- Use a line guide so that your writing doesn't slope up or down the form.

- Keep a photocopy of the application so that you can be well prepared if invited for an interview.

- Keep a record of all the job applications you have made, including the original advertisement.

- Look at the *TES* and *The Guardian* classified sections every week.

Job interviews and questions

To ask the hard question is simple
(W.H. Auden, Poems 1933)

It is vital that you create a positive impression at all stages of your interview.

- Dress appropriately.

- Be punctual.

- If you are shown around the school or introduced to prospective colleagues be observant, show an interest, ask relevant questions.

- Be aware of your body language at all times. Don't appear closed or uninterested.

- Prepare thoroughly for all interviews (see the questions on page 152). Many interviews begin with:

  'Tell us about yourself'

  'What can you offer this school'

  Rehearse answers to this kind of open-ended question.

- Refer to good practice in your answers, don't talk about unconnected theory.

- Some interviews are preceded by a presentation or a lesson. These can be stressful, but they are closer to the reality of teaching than an interview. If you are asked to give a talk or teach a lesson: prepare it, rehearse it, time it.

- Take with you to an interview examples of good work you have done – plans, handouts, analyses, reports, or whatever – show them if you can.

- It is worth applying for jobs for the interview practice. Then you will be ready for the one you really want.

- If you are unsuccessful, ask the interview panel for feedback.

Selection criteria

I have called this principle, by which each slight variation, if useful is preserved by the term Natural Selection
(Charles Darwin, Origin of Species)

1 Good appointment practice is to provide both a job and person specification.

2 The selection criteria for a post should be included in the information sent to you – ensure you demonstrate how to fulfil them.

3 If selection criteria are not provided it is reasonable to ask the interview panel how they will be making their decision.

4 Clearly, some schools will have 'hidden' criteria – such as a preference for appointing a woman, or someone who is a tough disciplinarian – which they may not want to make explicit. It is difficult to predict such criteria.

5 If you suspect that you have been discriminated against, remember that there are only two kinds of discrimination that are illegal:

- sexual discrimination
- racial/ethnic discrimination.

6 Some commonly used selection criteria are:

- relevant qualifications
- subject knowledge, including NC, examination syllabuses
- knowledge of relevant teaching techniques, materials
- administrative abilities, experience
- experience of work with or knowledge of this particular type of school
- experience or knowledge of the type of pupils at the school

- a commitment to LEA, school
- understanding the role of tutor
- contribution to school beyond the subject or phase
- ability to work with colleagues
- flexibility, initiative, enthusiasm
- if you were offered this post, would you be in a position to accept and take up the appointment within the time scale required?

Regular interview questions

- How did you find the school? (Both meanings of 'find'.)
- You've seen the school. Was it different to your expectations?
- What made you decide to become a teacher?
- What qualities do you have to enable you to become a successful teacher?
- Describe yourself in one word.
- What can you offer us that is different from the other candidates?
- Tell us about your PGCE course.
- Give a 5 minute presentation on positive aspects of your teaching practices.
- Tell us about your best lesson.
- Tell us about your worst lesson.
- What effect could the way a teacher or pupil dresses have on teaching and learning?
- Describe a good PSE lesson you have taught.
- What qualities do you think a tutor needs?
- What are your strengths?
- Are you well organised?
- What can you offer the school over and above being a class teacher?
- What is the greatest contribution you would make to this school?

- What are the ingredients of a good lesson?
- What are the main attributes of a good teacher?
- How would you deal with a badly behaved pupil?
- What would you consider important if you were involved in developing a policy of positive behaviour management?
- How would you cater for different abilities within the class?
- How would you plan for continuity and progression?
- How would you set up your new classroom?
- How would you plan for differentiation?
- How would you ensure each child in your class has access to their full curriculum entitlement?
- What initiatives have you seen that could benefit this school?
- Apart from subject lessons what other role should a school play in young people's lives?
- What methods would you use to motivate a child who simply refuses to respond in class?
- Do you think discipline is a more difficult issue with boys or girls? Would you deal with them differently?
- What strategies would you use to ensure equal opportunities within your classroom?
- What do you see as the role of the school in the community and how could you develop this?
- Tell us about your personal interests.
- How would you approach the teaching of reading?
- Do you feel parents are important, and why?
- What is the importance of teamwork in a school?
- Do you work well in a team?
- What are your curriculum strengths and your teaching strengths?
- What are your preferences for the area you would like to teach in, and which age range?
- What were your first impressions of this school?
- Why do you want to teach at this school?
- What changes have taken place in the teaching and learning of your subject over the last five years?
- We have an extensive range of extra-curricular activities here. In what ways could you contribute to these?

Chapter 7

Child protection

It is important that everyone working with children is aware of the signs of child abuse and is able to do something about it. Everyone who works in a school has contact with children. In many cases school staff may be the first adults to see children who have been abused. A class teacher has more opportunity to observe signs of abuse than other adults with whom the child has less contact.

Everyone, midday supervisors, secretaries, cooks, classroom assistants, caretakers or volunteers, has a duty to make sure that child abuse is dealt with immediately. All staff should follow LEA guidelines. Senior teachers and Child Protection Co-ordinators must be familiar with these guidelines.

Recognising signs of abuse or hearing a disclosure of abuse is always stressful. It can be convenient to decide there is no real evidence and do nothing. It is important to note that:

- boys and girls are abused
- abuse is never the child's fault
- children of all ages are abused
- child abuse can happen in all families

- women and men can be child abusers
- abuse gets worse until someone acts decisively
- most child abuse happens at home or in a 'safe' place
- in most sexual abuse cases the abuser is well known to the child.

> **Abuse – any child, any place at any time.**

School staff do not need to be able to define abuse in order to recognise it. However, definitions can be helpful as reference points to clarify your thinking. Child abuse can be described in four ways.

Physical abuse happens when children are physically hurt, injured or killed. Biting, burning, hitting, kicking, punching, shaking, slapping and squeezing are forms of abuse. Abuse also happens when children are given alcohol, inappropriate or illegal drugs and toxic substances.

Physical neglect is the result of children not being provided with their basic needs for survival. Physical neglect can include sub-standard accommodation, inappropriate food and drinks, poor clothing, lack of medical care and warmth, or leaving children alone and unsupervised.

Emotional abuse occurs when children suffer lack of confidence and self esteem. This is often brought about by lack of love and affection, or though shouting, taunts, threats and verbal attacks.

Sexual abuse takes place when children are used by adults for their own sexual gratification. This may include sexual intercourse, attempted sexual intercourse, anal intercourse, fondling, masturbation and oral sex. It also includes exposing children to or using them in the production of pornographic material.

> **Abuse or neglect – suspect it, report it.**

Recognising child abuse can be very difficult. Sometimes suspicions are no more than uncomfortable feelings. If you feel uneasy, talk to your Child Protection Co-ordinator (CPC). If the CPC is absent from school report your suspicions to the most senior member of staff available.

> **Make sure that you know who is your Child Protection Co-ordinator.**

Injuries or changes in behaviour may be the result of a number of things, including abuse. If you are uncomfortable, if you are uneasy, use the following guidelines to discreetly investigate your suspicions about **physical abuse**.

- Talk to the child about the injury, if you are at all unhappy with his explanation, discuss it with your CPC.
- Look at the position of the injury to see if it is in one of the common non-accidental injury sites.
- Bruises caused by shaking or squeezing will often show finger and thumb marks. Those caused by biting may be oval and open-ended.
- The size of a bite bruise may indicate whether it has been caused by an adult or another child.
- The reasons for facial bruising should always be looked into.
- Look carefully at burn marks and remember that cigarette burns are rarely caused by accident.
- Regular scald marks on buttocks, feet or hands are unlikely to have been caused by accidental splashing.

> **Abuse – if you are uneasy about an injury to a child, report it.**

The signs and symptoms of **physical neglect** are usually self-evident. Children may be:

- smelly
- often hungry
- failing to thrive
- constantly cold
- inappropriately dressed

> **If you notice signs of physical neglect, report them.**

Recognition of **sexual abuse** can be very difficult as physical signs may only be noticed when pupils undress. Indications of sexual abuse are more likely to be emotional or behavioural. Some signs are:

- eating disorders
- genital itching or pain
- difficulty with sitting or walking
- depression and suicide attempts
- unexplained changes in behaviour
- bloody, stained or torn underclothes
- reluctance to change clothes for games and swimming
- sexually explicit talk and behaviour inappropriate to the child's age.

Sexual abuse is more likely to be discovered by means of a disclosure either deliberate, accidental or through a third party.

Emotional abuse is probably the most difficult type of abuse to recognise. The signs are usually behavioural rather than physical. An emotionally abused child may:

- be a loner
- lack confidence
- be depressed
- have low self esteem
- thinks their work is 'rubbish'
- be withdrawn or introverted
- be used as a scapegoat by other children.

Report any unexplained change in a child's behaviour.

A pupil may choose to disclose to you that he or she has been abused. This will be a very stressful experience. The following guidelines may help you to deal with the **disclosure of abuse**.

- Always believe the child.
- Do not interrogate the child.
- Remain calm – be reassuring.

- Report any disclosures by third parties.
- Do not promise to keep the disclosure secret.
- Tell the child once more that you believe them.
- Tell the child that you are glad they have told you.
- Listen carefully and patiently to what the child has to say.
- Explain that you are going to have to report the disclosure.
- Report the disclosure as soon as possible to your Child Protection Co-ordinator or a senior member of staff.
- Do not discuss the disclosure with the child's parents or anyone else involved in the care of the child.
- Record the details of the disclosure and pass them on to the person you have reported it to.
- Treat sexually explicit drawings or stories produced in class as disclosure.
- If you suspect abuse from an overheard conversation treat it as disclosure.

If you have to deal with an emergency yourself do not take any action beyond that set out in your LEA procedures.

> **Delay could be fatal – never hold back for fear of making a mistake.**

Index